WHAT ARE THE BOOKS OF 1–2 CHRONICLES?

Kids' Guides to God's Word Series

What Is the Book of Genesis?
What Is the Book of Exodus?
What Is the Book of Leviticus?
What Is the Book of Numbers?
What Is the Book of Deuteronomy?
What Is the Book of Joshua?
What Is the Book of Judges?
What Is the Book of Ruth?
What Is the Book of 1 Samuel?
What Is the Book of 2 Samuel?
What Is the Book of 1 Kings?
What Is the Book of 2 Kings?
What Are the Books of 1–2 Chronicles?
What Are the Books of Ezra & Nehemiah?
What Is the Book of Esther?
What Is the Book of Job?
What Is the Book of Psalms?
What Is the Book of Proverbs?
What Is the Book of Ecclesiastes?
What Are the Books of Song of Songs & Lamentations?
What Is the Book of Isaiah?
What Is the Book of Jeremiah?
What Is the Book of Ezekiel?
What Is the Book of Daniel?
What Are the Books of Hosea–Micah?
What Are the Books of Nahum–Malachi?

What Is the Gospel of Matthew?
What Is the Gospel of Mark?
What Is the Gospel of Luke?
What Is the Gospel of John?
What Is the Book of Acts?
What Is the Book of Romans?
What Is the Book of 1 Corinthians?
What Is the Book of 2 Corinthians?
What Is the Book of Galatians?
What Is the Book of Ephesians?
What Is the Book of Philippians?
What Are the Books of Colossians & Philemon?
What Are the Books of 1–2 Thessalonians?
What Are the Books of 1–2 Timothy & Titus?
What Is the Book of Hebrews?
What Is the Book of James?
What Are the Books of 1–2 Peter & Jude?
What Are the Books of 1-3 John?
What Is the Book of Revelation?

What Are the Books of
1-2 CHRONICLES?

Michael Whitworth

ISBN 978-1-971767-22-2

Published by Start2Finish
Bend, Oregon 97702
start2finish.org

Printed in the United States of America
30 29 28 27 26   1 2 3 4 5

CONTENTS

INTRODUCTION

Have you ever watched a movie based on a true story and then watched a documentary about the same events? The movie gives you the drama—the battles, the betrayals, the big emotional moments. But the documentary gives you something different. It steps back and asks, "What did all of that actually mean? What were we supposed to learn? And what does it have to do with us right now?"

That's basically the difference between 1–2 Samuel and 1–2 Kings on the one hand and 1–2 Chronicles on the other. They cover much of the same history. Many of the same kings show up. Some of the same battles are fought. If you read Chronicles right after finishing Kings, you might wonder why the Bible bothers telling the story twice.

But Chronicles isn't a repeat. It's a retelling, and the difference matters. The Chronicler looked at the same events and asked different questions. He wasn't just recording what happened. He was showing his audience—a small, struggling community trying to rebuild their lives after exile—what it all meant and why it still mattered.

If Samuel and Kings are the movie, Chronicles is the documentary. Same history. Completely different purpose.

WHY WAS THIS BOOK WRITTEN?

Here's the situation. Around 539 BC, after decades of exile in Babylon, the people of Judah were allowed to go home. A Persian emperor named Cyrus issued a decree permitting them to return to Jerusalem and rebuild the temple. They went back, but what they found was devastating. The city was in ruins. The temple was rubble. The walls were broken. The once-glorious kingdom of David and Solomon was a pile of stones and ashes.

And these returning exiles had some big questions. Were they still God's people? Did the old promises still apply? Was there any point in rebuilding the temple, restarting worship, or organizing priests and Levites when everything felt so small and so broken?

The Chronicler wrote his book to answer those questions. His answer was a thundering *yes*. Yes, you are still God's people. Yes, the promises still hold. Yes, worship still matters. Yes, the line of David still has a future. Everything your ancestors built— the temple, the priesthood, the worship, the kingdom—was real, it was important, and it's worth rebuilding. God hasn't changed. His purposes haven't failed. And the invitation is still open.

WHAT MAKES CHRONICLES DIFFERENT?

If you've read 1–2 Samuel and 1–2 Kings, you'll notice some striking differences when you open Chronicles.

First, Chronicles skips what it doesn't need. There's almost nothing about Saul's reign, and the entire northern kingdom of Israel is largely ignored. The Chronicler wasn't interested in retelling every political detail. He cared about Judah, the Davidic line, and the temple, because those were the things that connected his readers to God's ongoing purposes.

Second, Chronicles adds material you won't find anywhere else. David's organization of the Levites, priests, and musicians. Jehoshaphat's battle won by a choir. Hezekiah's Passover inviting the northern tribes. And the stunning story of Manasseh—the worst king in Judah's history—repenting in chains and being restored by God. These stories, found only in Chronicles, carry some of the book's most powerful messages.

Third, Chronicles focuses on worship. The temple isn't just a building in this book—it's the center of everything. David prepares for it. Solomon builds it. Good kings restore it. Bad kings defile it. And when it's destroyed, the whole nation falls with it. For the Chronicler, worship isn't one part of life. It's the foundation of everything else.

Fourth, Chronicles traces a pattern. Over and over, the Chronicler shows what happens when kings seek God and what happens when they don't. Seek God, and he will be found. Forsake him, and he will forsake you. Humble yourself, and mercy comes. Refuse to humble yourself, and consequences follow. This pattern, rooted in God's promise to Solomon in 2 Chronicles 7:14, runs through the entire book like a heartbeat.

WHAT YOU'RE ABOUT TO READ

Here's where we're headed.

Chapter 1 covers the genealogies of 1 Chronicles 1–9. Before you skip them—don't. These lists of names are actually a story about identity, showing the returned exiles exactly who they are and where they came from.

Chapter 2 covers 1 Chronicles 10–16, from the death of Saul through David's bringing the ark to Jerusalem. You'll see how the Chronicler portrays David: not primarily as a warrior or politician but as a worshiper.

Chapter 3 covers 1 Chronicles 17–22, including God's covenant with David and the preparations for the temple. The Chronicler shows that David's greatest legacy wasn't his military victories but what he set in motion for God's house.

Chapter 4 covers 1 Chronicles 23–29, David's final act: organizing every detail of temple worship and giving away his personal fortune. These chapters, found entirely in Chronicles, reveal what mattered most to David at the end of his life.

Chapter 5 covers 2 Chronicles 1–7, from Solomon's request for wisdom through the temple dedication, including the moment when God's glory filled the house and fire fell from heaven—a detail only Chronicles records.

Chapter 6 covers 2 Chronicles 8–12, the height of Solomon's glory and the devastating split of the kingdom under his son Rehoboam, including the migration of faithful priests and Levites from the north—a story unique to Chronicles.

Chapter 7 covers 2 Chronicles 13–24, a parade of kings both faithful and faithless. You'll encounter Asa's desperate prayer against an impossible army, Jehoshaphat's choir marching ahead of his soldiers, and Joash's tragic reversal after his mentor died—all material unique to Chronicles.

Chapter 8 covers 2 Chronicles 25–36, the long descent into exile and the astonishing hope that emerges at the very end. Manasseh's repentance, Hezekiah's reunification Passover, and Cyrus' decree are among the most powerful stories in the book—and none of them appear in Kings.

WHY THIS BOOK MATTERS

You might be thinking, "OK, but I'm not an Israelite returning from exile. Why should I care about Chronicles?"

Because you've probably asked the same questions they asked. Does God still care about me? Is it too late to start over? Does what I do in worship actually matter? Can someone who's messed up as badly as I have really come back?

Chronicles answers every one of those questions. It says God's mercy is wider than you think. It says worship is more important than you realize. It says no one is beyond the reach of grace—not even Manasseh, the worst king who ever lived. It says the door is always open to anyone who humbles themselves and seeks God.

And it says something else, something the post-exilic community needed to hear and we need to hear too: the story isn't over. The last words of Chronicles are an invitation, not a funeral: "Any of his people among you—may the Lord their God be with them, and let them go up." Go up. Rebuild. Start again. God is with you.

BEFORE YOU BEGIN

A few things to keep in mind as you read.

The genealogies matter. They're long and full of unfamiliar names, but they're the Chronicler's way of saying, "You have a place in this story." Don't rush past them.

The repetition is intentional. If you notice the same themes showing up over and over—seeking God, humbling yourself, trusting him in battle, worshiping with your whole heart—that's not lazy writing. That's the Chronicler drilling the most important lessons into his readers' hearts.

The differences from Samuel and Kings are the point. When Chronicles tells the same story differently, pay attention. What the Chronicler adds, removes, or emphasizes reveals what he most wants you to understand.

This book points forward. David's throne. God's promise. The temple as a place where heaven meets earth. The invitation to all nations. Chronicles is pointing toward someone greater than David, greater than Solomon, greater than any king in Judah's line—a King whose throne really will last forever.

LET'S BEGIN

So here we are, about to open one of the most overlooked and underappreciated books in the Bible. We'll walk through genealogies that tell the story of a people. We'll watch David pour everything he had into a temple he'd never see. We'll stand in the cloud of God's glory as it fills Solomon's house. We'll march with Jehoshaphat's choir into an impossible battle. We'll watch a kingdom crack, crumble, and fall.

And then, in the final breath of the final chapter, we'll hear the most unlikely voice in Scripture—a Persian emperor—issue an invitation that still echoes today: come home. Rebuild. God is with you.

The story starts with a list of names. And the first name on the list is Adam.

Turn the page.

1

EVERY NAME HAS A STORY

Daniel Defoe's *Robinson Crusoe* tells the story of a man shipwrecked on a deserted island, completely alone, thousands of miles from home. For years, Crusoe has no contact with the world he came from. No family. No community. No proof that his old life ever existed. He builds a shelter, grows food, survives. But surviving isn't the same as belonging. One of the most haunting parts of the book is watching Crusoe struggle to remember who he is. He keeps a journal. He marks the days. He reads his Bible. He holds onto anything that connects him to the life he once knew, because without those connections, he's just a man on a rock in the middle of the ocean. Nobody. Nothing.

Now imagine an entire nation feeling that way.

That's where the story of 1–2 Chronicles begins. The people of Judah had been through the worst disaster in their history. The Babylonians had destroyed Jerusalem, torn down the temple, and dragged God's people into exile. For seventy years, they lived in a foreign land, surrounded by foreign gods, wondering if the promises God had made to Abraham, to Moses, to David still meant anything at all.

Then, finally, they were allowed to come home. A Persian emperor named Cyrus issued a decree: the Jews could return to their land and rebuild.

But the "home" they came back to didn't look like home. The city was in ruins. The temple was gone. There was no king on David's throne. They were a tiny, struggling community in a vast empire that didn't care about them. The Promised Land felt more like Robinson Crusoe's island than the kingdom of David and Solomon.

And into that situation, the Chronicler (the anonymous author of 1–2 Chronicles) did something that might surprise you. He didn't start with an action scene. He didn't open with a battle or a miracle or a dramatic rescue. He opened with a list of names.

Nine chapters of names.

If you've ever tried to read the first nine chapters of 1 Chronicles, you know the feeling. Name after name after name. Fathers and sons. Clans and tribes. It reads like the world's longest roll call. Most people hit chapter 1 and skip straight to chapter 10, where the actual story begins.

But here's the thing: those names *are* the story. Or at least, they're the foundation the entire story is built on.

The Chronicler wasn't writing a boring list. He was answering the most important question his community faced: *Who are we?* The people of Judah had lost almost everything that defined them. They had no king. They had no grand temple. They were a tiny province in someone else's empire. It would have been easy to look around and think, "We're nobody. We don't matter anymore. God has forgotten us."

The genealogies were the Chronicler's answer to that despair. He was saying: You are not nobody. You have a story that stretches all the way back to the beginning of the world. You belong to a plan that God has been unfolding since he created the first human being. And that plan is still going.

FROM ADAM TO ABRAHAM

The very first word of 1 Chronicles is "Adam." Not Abraham. Not Moses. Not David. Adam. The Chronicler starts at the very beginning of human history and draws a line, name by name, generation by generation, all the way to the people standing in the rubble of Jerusalem.

Think about what that means. The Chronicler could have started anywhere. He could have started with Abraham, the father of the nation. He could have started with Moses, who led the exodus. But he started with Adam, the first human being, the man God formed from the dust and placed in a garden. Why?

Because he wanted his readers to understand that God's plan didn't start with Israel. It started with *everyone*. The whole world belongs to God. Every nation, every people group, every family traced back to the same source. The Chronicler lists the descendants of Noah's three sons—Japheth, Ham, and Shem— and in doing so, he creates a kind of map of the ancient world. All the nations are there. All of them are part of God's creation.

But then the focus narrows. Out of all those nations, God chose one family to carry his promises forward. The line runs from Adam to Noah, from Noah to Shem, from Shem to Abraham. Ten generations from Adam to Noah. Ten generations from Shem to Abraham. The numbers aren't accidental. They create a rhythm, a sense of purpose. History isn't random. It's going somewhere.

And notice how the Chronicler handles the family tree. When he lists Noah's sons, he deals with Japheth first, then Ham, then Shem—saving the most important line for last. When he gets to Abraham's sons, he lists Ishmael's descendants first, then Esau's, saving Israel for last. Every time, the secondary lines are cleared away so the spotlight can fall on the line of promise.

It's like a camera slowly zooming in. The wide shot shows the whole world. Then it narrows to one region. Then one family. Then one nation. The Chronicler is telling his readers: out of all the people on earth, God chose you. Not because you're better than everyone else. Not because you earned it. But because God made a promise, and he keeps his promises.

THE TRIBE THAT MATTERS MOST

Once the Chronicler reaches the twelve sons of Israel, something interesting happens. He doesn't give equal space to every tribe. Judah gets far more attention than anyone else—chapters 2–4 are almost entirely devoted to Judah's descendants. Levi, the priestly tribe, gets a long section too. Little Benjamin gets more coverage than you'd expect. But some tribes barely get a verse.

Why the imbalance? Because the Chronicler isn't trying to be fair. He's trying to make a point.

Judah matters because this is the tribe that produced David, and David's royal line was the focus of God's greatest promises about the future. The Chronicler traces the line from

Judah through Perez (born from a scandalous situation involving Judah and his daughter-in-law Tamar) to Jesse and then to David. He even lists David's descendants all the way through the exile and beyond, showing that the royal line survived. The family of David wasn't extinct. The promise was still alive.

And here's something worth noticing: Judah's family tree is the most ethnically diverse of all the tribes. Tucked into the genealogy you'll find a Canaanite woman (the daughter of Shua, who married Judah himself), an Ishmaelite (Jether, the father of Amasa), and an Egyptian servant (Jarha, who married into the family of Jerahmeel). The line that would produce David—and eventually the Messiah—was not a pure bloodline. It included outsiders. Foreigners. People you wouldn't expect to find in the family tree of Israel's greatest king.

The Chronicler doesn't hide this. He puts it right there in the record. It's as if he's saying: God's plan has always been bigger than one nation. It has always included people from the outside.

A MAN NAMED "PAIN"

Buried in the middle of these genealogies, the Chronicler drops in a tiny story that has nothing to do with lineage and everything to do with faith. It's only two verses long, but it's one of the most memorable passages in the entire book.

His name was Jabez. His mother named him that because she gave birth to him in great pain, and the name basically meant "pain." Imagine going through life with a name like that. Every time someone called you, they were calling you "Pain." Every time you introduced yourself, you were announcing your own misfortune.

But Jabez didn't accept what his name said about him. He prayed. "Oh, that you would bless me and enlarge my territory! Let your hand be with me, and keep me from harm so that I will be free from pain." And God granted his request.

That's it. Two verses. But the Chronicler put this story here on purpose. Right in the middle of a list of names—most of whom we know nothing about—he placed a man who refused to be defined by his circumstances and cried out to God instead. For a community that felt defined by loss and failure, Jabez was a reminder: your name doesn't have to be your destiny. God answers prayer. He can turn pain into blessing.

THE PRIESTS WHO KEPT THE FIRE BURNING

The tribe of Levi gets an enormous amount of space in the genealogies—almost all of chapter 6. That might seem strange until you remember what the Levites did. They were the priests and worship leaders of Israel. They served in the temple. They offered sacrifices. They led the people in praising God.

For the Chronicler's community, this mattered more than almost anything else. They no longer had a king. The Davidic dynasty was over, at least for now. But they did have priests. They did have worship. The temple had been rebuilt (even if it was smaller and less impressive than Solomon's original). And the Chronicler wanted his readers to understand that the worship system—the priesthood, the singers, the gatekeepers—stretched all the way back through Israel's history in an unbroken line.

The Levites represented continuity. They were living proof that God's relationship with his people hadn't been severed by the exile. The fire on the altar might have gone out when

Babylon destroyed the temple, but now it was burning again. The same families who had served God for generations were still serving him. The thread had not been cut.

CHAPTER 9: THE THREAD HOLDS

The genealogies end with chapter 9, and this chapter is the whole point. After eight chapters of tracing Israel's history from Adam through the monarchy, the Chronicler arrives at his own time: the community that returned from exile and resettled in Jerusalem.

He mentions the exile in a single sentence. "Judah was taken into exile in Babylon because of their unfaithfulness." That's it. No lengthy description of the destruction. No detailed account of the horrors they suffered. The Chronicler treats the exile almost like a parenthesis—something that happened, yes, but something that is now behind them.

What matters is what comes next: "Now the first to resettle on their own property in their own towns were some Israelites, priests, Levites, and temple servants."

They came back. They resettled. They started again.

And notice who's included. The chapter lists people from Judah and Benjamin, which you'd expect. Those were the tribes of the southern kingdom. But it also mentions people from Ephraim and Manasseh, tribes from the northern kingdom that had been conquered by Assyria over a century before Babylon destroyed Jerusalem. The Chronicler is hinting at something he deeply hoped for: that the returned community wasn't just a fragment of the old southern kingdom. It was the beginning of a restored *whole* Israel—all twelve tribes, drawn back together.

The chapter goes on to describe the temple workers in detail. Gatekeepers. Singers. People who baked the bread for the offerings. People who mixed the spices for the incense. People who opened the doors of the temple every morning. These aren't glamorous jobs. Nobody writes songs about the guy who unlocked the temple doors at dawn. But the Chronicler lists them by name, because every one of them was part of keeping Israel's worship alive.

WHAT THIS MEANS FOR US

First, your story is part of a bigger story. The genealogies remind us that no one exists in isolation. Every person in those lists was connected to a family, a tribe, a nation, and ultimately to God's plan for the entire world. The same is true for you. Your life isn't random. It's connected to something much larger than you can see. God has been working across generations, and your story is part of his.

Second, God doesn't forget his people, even when everything falls apart. The community that returned from exile looked nothing like the Israel of David and Solomon. They were small, weak, and struggling. But God hadn't abandoned them. The genealogies were proof: the line continued. The promises still stood. If you're going through a season where everything seems broken, the genealogies of Chronicles are a reminder that God is faithful across centuries. He doesn't quit.

Third, your circumstances don't define you. Jabez was named "Pain," but he didn't let that name become his future. He prayed, and God answered. Whatever label the world has stuck on you—whether it's "not good enough" or "too different" or "not important"—God can rewrite that story. The question is whether you'll bring it to him.

Fourth, the "boring" parts of faithfulness matter. Most of the names in these nine chapters belong to people who never did anything famous. They lived, they raised families, they passed on the faith, and they died. But without them, the line would have broken. The promise would have been lost. The unglamorous, everyday faithfulness of ordinary people is what holds God's plan together. You don't have to be David or Solomon to matter. You just have to be faithful where you are.

TALKING POINTS

1. **The genealogies start with Adam, not Abraham.** Why do you think the Chronicler wanted to connect Israel's story all the way back to the beginning of creation? What does that say about how God sees every nation and every person?

2. **Jabez refused to accept that his painful name would define his life, and he prayed boldly to God for something better.** What are some "labels" that people carry today—things others have said about them or circumstances they were born into—that feel like they define who they are? How does Jabez's example challenge that?

3. **The Chronicler gave enormous attention to the Levites and the details of temple worship—gatekeepers, singers, people who baked bread and mixed incense.** Why do you think those "behind the scenes" roles mattered so much to him? What are some behind-the-scenes roles in your church or community that don't get much attention but are essential?

4. The returned community was small, weak, and nothing like the Israel of David and Solomon. But the Chronicler told them they were the continuation of God's plan stretching back to Adam. How does knowing you're part of a bigger story—one that started long before you and will continue after you—change how you see your own life and struggles?

5. Judah's family tree included outsiders: a Canaanite woman, an Ishmaelite, an Egyptian servant. What does it tell you about God's character that he wove foreigners into the most important family line in Israel? How does this connect to the message of the gospel?

The genealogies are finished. Nine chapters of names, stretching from the first man who ever lived to the small community huddled around a rebuilt temple in Jerusalem. It might have looked like the end. It felt like an afterthought.

But the Chronicler saw something different. He saw the thread of God's faithfulness running through every generation, unbroken, unstoppable. And now it was time to tell the story of the king who, more than anyone else, showed Israel what faithfulness to God could look like.

His name was David. And his story was about to begin.

Turn the page.

2

WHEN WORSHIP CAME HOME

Alexandre Dumas's *The Three Musketeers* tells the story of a young man named d'Artagnan who travels to Paris with almost nothing—no money, no connections, no reputation. He's an outsider. Nobody takes him seriously. But one by one, he wins the loyalty of three of the most skilled swordsmen in France: Athos, Porthos, and Aramis. They come from different backgrounds and have different personalities, but they rally around d'Artagnan because they believe in him. Their motto becomes one of the most famous lines in literature: "All for one, and one for all." By the end of the story, what looked like a ragtag group of misfits has become an unstoppable force—not because of any single fighter's ability, but because they chose to unite behind the same cause.

Something very similar happens in 1 Chronicles 10–16. A failed king dies in disgrace. A shepherd-turned-fugitive steps into the spotlight. And then, in one of the most remarkable scenes in the entire Bible, warriors from every single tribe in Israel—including the dead king's own tribe—show up to declare their loyalty. Mighty men. Archers. Lion-faced soldiers.

Commanders of thousands. They come from the north and the south, from the east and the west, pouring into Hebron like rivers flowing to the sea.

"All for one, and one for all" could have been their motto too.

But here's where Chronicles takes the story somewhere unexpected. The Chronicler isn't mainly interested in David the warrior or David the king. He's interested in David the worshiper. The real climax of these chapters isn't a battle won or a city conquered. It's a golden box carried on the shoulders of priests, a choir singing at the top of their lungs, and a king dancing in the streets of Jerusalem.

This is the story of how worship came home.

THE KING WHO FAILED

The Chronicler doesn't ease into David's story. He opens with a dead body on a battlefield.

First Chronicles 10 tells the story of Saul's final day. The Philistines attacked Israel on Mount Gilboa. Saul's three sons—including Jonathan, David's closest friend—were killed. Saul himself was badly wounded by archers. Rather than be captured and humiliated by his enemies, he fell on his own sword.

The next day, the Philistines found the bodies. They stripped Saul's armor, cut off his head, and sent messengers throughout their territory to spread the news. They hung Saul's head in the temple of their god Dagon and put his armor in the temple of their idols, as if their gods had won the victory.

If you've read 1 Samuel, you know this story. But Chronicles adds something that Samuel doesn't. After describing

Saul's death, the Chronicler steps back and explains *why* it happened:

"Saul died because he was unfaithful to the Lord; he did not keep the word of the Lord and even consulted a medium for guidance, and did not inquire of the Lord. So the Lord put him to death and turned the kingdom over to David son of Jesse."

That's the Chronicler's verdict, and it sets the tone for everything that follows. The word "unfaithful" is one of the most important words in all of Chronicles. It's the word the Chronicler uses to explain why kingdoms rise and fall, why blessings come and go, why exile happened. And the opposite of unfaithfulness? Seeking God. Inquiring of the Lord. That's exactly what Saul failed to do—and exactly what David will do.

The contrast is sharp and deliberate. Saul didn't seek God. David will. And that single difference changes everything.

EVERYONE SHOWS UP

What happens next is one of the most unique sections in all of Chronicles—material you won't find anywhere in 1 or 2 Samuel.

First Chronicles 11 tells us that all Israel gathered at Hebron to make David king. The people acknowledged what God had already declared: David was meant to shepherd Israel. They anointed him, and he was king.

But then the Chronicler does something unexpected. Instead of rushing forward into David's reign, he hits pause and looks backward. Chapter 12 is an entire chapter—found only in Chronicles—devoted to listing the warriors who had come to David's side during the dark years when he was a fugitive running from Saul.

Think about what that means. While David was hiding in caves and living in enemy territory, while it looked like Saul would hunt him down and kill him, people were quietly choosing sides. And they were choosing David.

Warriors from Benjamin—Saul's own tribe—showed up at Ziklag, skilled with bows and slings, able to shoot with both hands. Soldiers from Gad crossed the Jordan during flood season to reach David in the wilderness. The text describes them as men whose "faces were the faces of lions" and who "were as swift as gazelles in the mountains." Men from Judah and Benjamin came to David's hideout, and when David asked if they came in peace, a man named Amasai was filled with God's Spirit and declared, "We are yours, David! We are with you, son of Jesse! Peace, peace to you, and peace to your helpers! For your God helps you."

Did you catch the theme? Help. The word "help" echoes through the entire chapter like a drumbeat. God was helping David—and he was doing it through people. Ordinary men from ordinary tribes who decided that David was worth following, even when following him was dangerous.

The chapter builds toward a massive gathering at Hebron. The Chronicler lists the numbers: 6,800 from Judah. 7,100 from Simeon. 4,600 from Levi. 3,000 from Benjamin. 20,800 from Ephraim. 18,000 from the western half of Manasseh. The list goes on and on. From the tribe of Issachar came "men who understood the times and knew what Israel should do." From Zebulun came 50,000 experienced soldiers, loyal and united.

Add it all up and you get a picture the Chronicler

desperately wanted his readers to see: all Israel, united under one king, with one purpose.

The chapter ends with a celebration that sounds more like a feast than a military assembly. People came from as far away as Issachar, Zebulun, and Naphtali, bringing food on donkeys, camels, mules, and oxen—flour, fig cakes, raisin cakes, wine, olive oil, cattle, and sheep. The final sentence says it all: "There was joy in Israel."

For the Chronicler's original audience—a small, struggling community in post-exilic Jerusalem—this picture must have been electrifying. All twelve tribes. United. Joyful. Rallying behind God's chosen king. It was a reminder of what Israel was meant to be. And a promise of what it could be again.

THE DAY EVERYTHING WENT WRONG

David's first major act as king wasn't building a palace or launching a military campaign. It was seeking God.

He decided to bring the ark of the covenant to Jerusalem. The ark was the most sacred object in all of Israel—a gold-covered wooden chest that held the stone tablets of the Ten Commandments. More importantly, it was the place where God's presence dwelt, enthroned above two golden angels. The ark represented something profound: God living among his people.

During Saul's entire reign, the ark had sat neglected in an obscure village called Kiriath Jearim. Nobody paid attention to it. Nobody sought God's presence through it. David wanted to change that. He assembled all Israel, and with great celebration—singing, harps, lyres, tambourines, cymbals, trumpets—they set out to bring the ark home to Jerusalem.

But something went terribly wrong.

They transported the ark on a cart pulled by oxen, the way the Philistines had once sent it back to Israel. When the oxen stumbled at a threshing floor, a man named Uzzah reached out to steady the ark. And God struck him dead.

The celebration stopped. The music died. David was angry, then afraid. "How can I ever bring the ark of God to me?" he asked. He left the ark at the house of a man named Obed-Edom and went home.

This story shocks modern readers. Uzzah was trying to help. Why would God kill him for that?

The answer lies in what David later realized: they had done it wrong. God had given specific instructions for how the ark was to be moved. It was supposed to be carried on poles by Levites—priests from the tribe of Levi who had been set apart for this task. No one else was supposed to touch it. The ark wasn't just a box. It was the throne of the living God. And God's holiness isn't something you approach casually, no matter how good your intentions are.

David learned a hard lesson that day. Enthusiasm for God is not the same as obedience to God. Good intentions don't replace doing things God's way.

THE DAY EVERYTHING WENT RIGHT

Three months later, David tried again. But this time, he did it differently.

First Chronicles 15 records preparations that don't appear in 2 Samuel's version of the story. David gathered the Levites and told them plainly: "It was because you, the Levites, did not bring it up the first time that the Lord our God broke out in anger against us. We did not inquire of him about how to do it in the prescribed way."

This time, the Levites consecrated themselves. They carried the ark on their shoulders with poles, exactly as Moses had commanded. And the Chronicler devotes verse after verse to something 2 Samuel barely mentions: the music.

David appointed Levites as singers and musicians. He organized them into groups with specific instruments—bronze cymbals, harps, lyres. He appointed a music director named Kenaniah, who led the singing because "he was skillful at it." He stationed gatekeepers and trumpet players. He didn't just want the ark moved correctly. He wanted the moment to be glorious.

And it was. When the Levites successfully lifted the ark and began to carry it, sacrifices were offered in thanksgiving. David, wearing a linen robe, danced before God with all his might. The sound of shouting, trumpets, cymbals, harps, and lyres filled the air. The ark of God entered Jerusalem, and the whole nation celebrated.

THE SONG THAT SAID EVERYTHING

But the Chronicler still wasn't finished. In chapter 16, he includes something that 2 Samuel's account doesn't have at all: a psalm.

After the ark was placed inside the tent David had prepared, after the burnt offerings and fellowship offerings were made, after David blessed the people and gave everyone bread and raisin cakes, he appointed Asaph and his fellow Levites to lead the nation in a song of thanksgiving. The psalm that follows draws from three different psalms in our book of Psalms (Psalms 105, 96, and 106), woven together into one sweeping hymn.

The song starts with gratitude: "Give praise to the Lord, proclaim his name; make known among the nations what he has done. Sing to him, sing praise to him; tell of all his wonderful acts."

Then it moves to memory: "Remember the wonders he has done, his miracles, and the judgments he pronounced." The psalm walks through God's covenant with Abraham, his protection of the patriarchs, and his faithfulness across the generations. For people who had just read the genealogies of chapters 1–9, these words connected everything. The same God who made promises to Abraham was now being worshiped in Jerusalem.

Then the song expands to the whole world: "Sing to the Lord, all the earth; proclaim his salvation day after day. Declare his glory among the nations, his marvelous deeds among all peoples."

And it ends with a prayer: "Save us, God our Savior; gather us and deliver us from the nations, so that we may give thanks to your holy name, and glory in your praise."

For the Chronicler's audience—a small group of returned exiles in a rebuilt Jerusalem—that prayer wasn't ancient history. It was their daily reality. They needed saving. They needed gathering. They needed deliverance. And the psalm reminded them that the God who had always saved his people was still their God.

David left Asaph and his fellow Levites to minister before the ark continually. He appointed musicians and gatekeepers to serve at the tent. He stationed Zadok the priest at the tabernacle in Gibeon to offer the daily sacrifices. Worship wasn't a one-time event. It was an ongoing, organized, daily reality at the center of Israel's life.

The people went home. David went home to bless his family. And for the first time in a very long time, worship had a home too.

WHAT THIS MEANS FOR US

First, how you approach God matters as much as whether you approach him. David's first attempt to bring the ark to Jerusalem was motivated by genuine devotion. But good intentions weren't enough. God had given specific instructions, and David had ignored them. When he obeyed—when he did things God's way instead of his own—everything changed. Sincerity matters, but sincerity is not a substitute for obedience.

Second, God builds his kingdom through people who show up. Chapter 12 is a whole chapter about people who chose to support David when it was risky and unpopular. God didn't establish David's kingdom through angels or miracles. He did it through ordinary people who showed up at the right time with willing hearts. The same is true today. God's work in the world advances through people who are willing to be part of something bigger than themselves.

Third, worship isn't an add-on—it's the point. The Chronicler could have focused on David's military victories or his political achievements. Instead, the climax of these chapters is a worship service. The song. The musicians. The priests. The daily ministry before the ark. For the Chronicler, the most important thing a king could do wasn't conquer enemies. It was lead his people in worshiping God. If that was true for a king, it's true for us too.

Fourth, unity comes from seeking God together. The picture of all Israel gathering with "one mind" to make David king, then celebrating together as the ark entered Jerusalem, is a picture of what God's people are supposed to look like. Not divided by tribe or background, but united in purpose. When God's people seek him together, something powerful happens. Joy follows.

TALKING POINTS

1. **The Chronicler says Saul died because he was "unfaithful" and "did not inquire of the Lord."** What does it look like to "inquire of the Lord" in your daily life? Why do you think seeking God is such a central idea in Chronicles?

2. **Warriors from Saul's own tribe of Benjamin came to support David.** Why is that surprising? Have you ever had to support someone or something that went against what the people closest to you expected?

3. **The Uzzah story shows that good intentions aren't enough—God cares about how we approach him, not just that we approach him.** How does this balance with the idea that God is loving and welcoming? Can both be true at the same time?

4. **David organized the Levites as full-time musicians, singers, and worship leaders.** What does it tell you about God that he wanted excellence and beauty in worship, not just obedience? How should this shape the way we think about worship today?

5. The psalm in chapter 16 calls the whole earth to sing to the Lord and declares his glory "among the nations." Why do you think worship and mission are so closely connected in the Bible? How does worshiping God change the way we see the rest of the world?

David had brought the ark to Jerusalem. He had organized worship. He had united the nation. The king who sought God was seeing God's promises unfold before his eyes.

But David wasn't finished. He had one more dream—a dream so big that God himself would have to weigh in on it. David wanted to build God a permanent house. A temple. And God's response to that dream would become the most important promise in the entire Old Testament.

Turn the page.

3

THE BIGGER PROMISE

There's a moment in *Incredibles 2* that Bob Parr—Mr. Incredible—absolutely hates. For the first time in his superhero career, he isn't the one going on the mission. His wife, Helen, is. She's the one saving the city, making headlines, and changing the world. Bob's job? Stay home. Watch the kids. Help with homework. Change diapers.

He's terrible at it. Not because the work is beneath him, but because every fiber of his being screams that he should be out there doing the heroic thing himself. He knows he's strong enough. He knows he's capable enough. But the mission isn't his this time. It's Helen's. And the hardest thing Mr. Incredible has ever done isn't punching a villain. It's supporting someone else's mission when he wanted it to be his own.

David knew exactly how that felt.

After everything he had done—uniting the tribes, bringing the ark to Jerusalem, establishing worship, defeating every enemy God put in front of him—David had one dream left. The big one. He wanted to build God a house. A permanent temple to replace the tent where the ark sat. A structure worthy of the God who had given him everything.

God said no.

Not because David had done something wrong. Not because God was punishing him. But because the mission wasn't David's. It belonged to his son. And the hardest thing David ever did wasn't killing a giant or conquering a city. It was accepting that his greatest contribution to God's kingdom would be preparing for something he would never see finished.

First Chronicles 17–22 tell that story. And tucked inside it is the most important promise God ever made to a human king.

THE NIGHT GOD FLIPPED THE SCRIPT

David was settled in his cedar palace, the ark was in Jerusalem, and the kingdom was at peace. One evening, David shared an idea with the prophet Nathan: "Here I am, living in a house of cedar, while the ark of the covenant of the Lord is under a tent."

The implication was obvious. David lived in a palace. God lived in a tent. That didn't seem right. David wanted to build something magnificent for God, a permanent house of worship that would reflect God's glory to the nations.

Nathan's first response was encouraging: "Whatever you have in mind, do it, for God is with you." But that night, God spoke to Nathan with a different message. And what God said changed everything.

"You are not the one to build me a house to dwell in," God told Nathan. But then came the twist—one of the most stunning reversals in the Bible. David wanted to build God a house. God responded by promising to build David a house. The same word, "house," but with two completely different meanings. David was thinking of a building. God was talking about a dynasty, a family line that would last forever.

"When your days are over and you go to be with your ancestors," God said, "I will raise up your offspring to succeed you, one of your own sons, and I will establish his kingdom. He is the one who will build a house for me, and I will establish his throne forever. I will be his father, and he will be my son. I will never take my love away from him. I will set him over my house and my kingdom forever; his throne will be established forever."

Count the word "forever" in that passage. It appears again and again, like a bell being struck. God wasn't just promising David a son who would build a temple. He was promising a kingdom without end. A throne that would never be empty. A dynasty that would outlast every empire on earth.

And here's something the Chronicler emphasizes that 2 Samuel doesn't: in Chronicles, God calls the kingdom "my house and my kingdom." Not David's. God's. The Davidic king wouldn't just rule over Israel. He would sit on God's own throne, ruling over God's own kingdom. David was being told that his descendant would reign as God's representative over God's people forever.

No wonder David was speechless.

"WHO AM I?"

After Nathan delivered the message, David went and sat before the Lord. The text gives us a private moment—no audience, no officials, just a king alone with his God. And the first words out of his mouth were: "Who am I, Lord God, and what is my family, that you have brought me this far?"

This was the shepherd boy from Bethlehem. The youngest of eight brothers. The one his own father didn't bother to bring in when the prophet came looking for a king. And now God was promising him an eternal dynasty, a kingdom that would never end, a son who would sit on God's own throne.

David's prayer is one of the most beautiful in the Bible. He praised God for his uniqueness: "There is no one like you, Lord, and there is no God but you." He remembered what God had done for Israel: the exodus from Egypt, the covenant, the protection across the centuries. And he asked God to do exactly what he had promised: "Now, Lord, let the promise you have made concerning your servant and his house be established forever. Do as you promised."

David didn't negotiate. He didn't try to convince God to let him build the temple anyway. He accepted God's plan and asked for one thing: that God would keep his word.

That's faith. Not getting what you want, but trusting the one who knows what's best.

THE WARS THAT HAD TO BE WON

Chapters 18–20 record David's military victories in rapid succession. The Philistines, the Moabites, the Arameans, the Edomites, the Ammonites—one enemy after another fell before David's armies. The Chronicler repeats a simple refrain: "The Lord gave David victory wherever he went."

These chapters serve several purposes in the Chronicler's telling of the story. They show God fulfilling his promise to subdue David's enemies. They explain where all the gold, silver, bronze, and iron came from that David would later pour into temple preparations. And they explain something the Chronicler reveals later: why David couldn't build the temple himself. He had "shed much blood" and "fought many wars." God's house would be built by a man of peace, not a man of war.

There's something worth noticing about what the Chronicler *doesn't* include in these chapters. If you've read 2 Samuel, you know that right in the middle of David's wars, one of the darkest episodes in his life took place: his adultery with Bathsheba and the murder of her husband Uriah. It's one of the most devastating stories in the Bible.

The Chronicler doesn't tell it. Not because he didn't know about it. Everyone knew about it. But because his purpose was different. He wasn't writing a biography of David. He was showing his readers what faithful kingship could accomplish, and he was pointing forward to a greater king still to come. The Chronicler's silence about Bathsheba isn't a cover-up. It's a choice to focus on God's grace and David's legacy rather than his worst failure. Even after that terrible sin, God didn't abandon David. The story kept going. The promise still stood.

For the Chronicler's audience, struggling in their small post-exilic community, that was a message of hope: God uses imperfect people. Your worst failure doesn't cancel God's plan.

THE WORST DAY THAT LED TO THE BEST PLACE

Then came the census. First Chronicles 21 opens with a sentence that stops you cold: "Satan rose up against Israel and incited David to take a census of Israel." This is one of the few places in the Old Testament where Satan appears by name as a spiritual adversary. In the parallel account in 2 Samuel, the text says the Lord's anger burned against Israel and he incited David. Chronicles names the behind-the-scenes enemy: Satan himself.

Why was a census sinful? Because David wasn't counting the people to organize worship or plan for the future. He was counting his army. He wanted to know how many soldiers he had, and the implication was clear to everyone, including his general Joab. David was putting his trust in military strength instead of God.

Joab pushed back: "May the Lord multiply his troops a hundred times over. But why does my lord want to do this? Why should he bring guilt on Israel?"

David insisted. The count came back: over a million fighting men. But the pride that prompted the census brought a devastating consequence. God sent a plague on Israel, and seventy thousand people died.

Then David saw something terrifying: an angel standing between heaven and earth, sword stretched over Jerusalem, ready to destroy the city. David fell to the ground in sackcloth and cried out to God: "I am the one who sinned and did wrong. These are but sheep. What have they done? Let your hand fall on me and my family, but do not let this plague remain on your people."

God relented. The angel stopped. And then the prophet Gad told David to build an altar on the spot where the angel had stood, the threshing floor of a Jebusite named Araunah.

Here's where the story takes a remarkable turn. Araunah saw David coming and offered to give him everything: the land, the oxen for sacrifice, the wood for fuel. Free of charge.

David refused. "I will not take for the Lord what is yours, or sacrifice a burnt offering that costs me nothing."

David paid full price. He built the altar. He offered sacrifices. And God answered with fire from heaven, consuming the offering and commanding the angel to put away his sword.

The Chronicler wants you to see the connection. This threshing floor—the place where judgment stopped and mercy began—would become the site of Solomon's temple. The very spot where David's worst moment met God's grace would become the holiest place in Israel. When Solomon broke ground on the temple years later, 2 Chronicles 3:1 identifies the location precisely: "on Mount Moriah, where the Lord had appeared to his father David. It was on the threshing floor of Araunah the Jebusite."

God turned disaster into destiny. The place of David's deepest failure became the place of Israel's greatest worship.

PREPARING FOR WHAT HE'D NEVER SEE

Chapter 22 is entirely unique to Chronicles. You won't find a single verse of it in 1 or 2 Samuel. And it reveals something extraordinary about David's character.

After identifying the temple site, David threw himself into preparations. He gathered stonecutters and put them to work shaping dressed stone. He stockpiled iron for nails and fittings. He arranged for massive shipments of cedar logs from the Phoenician cities of Sidon and Tyre. He accumulated gold, silver, bronze, and iron in quantities so vast the text says they were "too great to be weighed."

All of this for a building he would never construct.

Then David called his son Solomon and gave him one of the most important speeches in the Bible. He explained why the temple wasn't his to build. God had said to David: "You have shed much blood and have fought many wars. You are not to build a house for my Name, because you have shed much blood on the earth in my sight. But you will have a son who will be a man of peace and rest. His name will be Solomon, and I will grant Israel peace and quiet during his reign. He is the one who will build a house for my Name."

David's wars had been necessary. They had fulfilled God's promises and established peace in the land. But the very thing that made David great as a warrior made him unsuitable as a temple builder. The house of God needed to be built by hands that represented peace, not war.

Then David spoke words over Solomon that echo all the way back to Moses and Joshua: "Be strong and courageous. Do not be afraid or discouraged."

David wasn't just giving Solomon a construction project. He was passing on a mission. And he was reminding his son that the same God who had been with Moses, with Joshua, and with David himself would be with Solomon too.

Finally, David turned to the leaders of Israel and told them to help his son. "Set your hearts and souls to seek the Lord your God," he commanded. Build the sanctuary. Bring the ark and the sacred vessels into a house built for the name of the Lord.

David would die before the first stone of the temple was laid. But everything Solomon needed would be ready.

WHAT THIS MEANS FOR US

First, God's promises are always bigger than we expect. David wanted to build God a building. God promised David an eternal kingdom. We tend to think small—a better grade, a closer friendship, a problem solved. God thinks in terms of eternity. His plans for your life are bigger than the box you're trying to put them in.

Second, not every calling is glamorous, but every calling matters. David didn't get to build the temple. He got to prepare for it. He gathered materials, organized workers, secured resources, and passed on wisdom. None of that made headlines. But without David's preparation, Solomon's temple never would have existed. Sometimes the most important work you do is work that someone else gets credit for.

Third, God brings good out of our worst moments. The threshing floor where David's sin brought judgment became the site of the temple where Israel worshiped for centuries. God doesn't waste our failures. When we repent, he can turn the place of our greatest shame into the place of our deepest worship.

Fourth, real generosity costs something. David refused to give God something that cost him nothing. That principle still holds. Worship that doesn't cost you anything—your time, your comfort, your pride, your resources—isn't really worship. God doesn't want your leftovers. He wants your best.

TALKING POINTS

1. David wanted to build God a temple, but God said no and offered something bigger instead: an eternal dynasty.

Have you ever had a dream or plan that God redirected? How did it turn out differently than you expected?

2. **David's prayer in chapter 17 begins with "Who am I?"** Why do you think David responded to God's incredible promise with humility rather than excitement? What does his response teach us about how to receive blessings from God?

3. **The Chronicler skips the story of David and Bathsheba and focuses instead on God's faithfulness despite David's imperfections.** What does it say about God's character that he keeps working through people even after they fail badly?

4. **David told Araunah, "I will not sacrifice a burnt offering that costs me nothing."** What does that statement mean for how we approach worship, giving, and serving God? What are some ways people today might try to give God something that costs them nothing?

5. **David spent his final years preparing for a temple he would never see completed.** What does his example teach us about investing in the next generation? How can you contribute to something that matters even if you won't be around to see the results?

Everything was in place. The promise had been made. The site had been chosen. The materials had been gathered. The charge had been given. David had done everything a father and a king could do to set up the next generation for success.

Now it was time to pass the torch—and to show one last time what it looked like to give everything you had to the God who had given you everything first.

Turn the page.

4

EVERYTHING HE HAD

Near the end of Disney's *Tarzan*, something happens that changes everything. Kerchak, the silverback gorilla who has led and protected the family for years, is mortally wounded. He's spent the entire film keeping Tarzan at arm's length—suspicious, guarded, never fully accepting this strange creature who didn't look like the rest of the family. But in his final moments, Kerchak looks at Tarzan and says the words he never said before: "Take care of them… my son." With those words, everything Kerchak built, everything he fought for, everything he protected, passes to the next generation. The old leader dies. The new one steps forward. And the family goes on.

That scene captures something real about how legacies work. The most important thing a leader does often isn't what he builds for himself. It's what he puts in place so the next person can succeed.

The last seven chapters of 1 Chronicles are David's version of that scene. These chapters exist only in Chronicles. You won't find any of this material in 1 or 2 Samuel. The Chronicler devoted nearly a quarter of David's entire story to something most people wouldn't consider exciting: organizing Levites, assigning priests to rotating schedules, setting up musician divisions, appointing gatekeepers and treasurers, and handing over architectural blueprints.

Then, at the very end, David stood before the whole nation, emptied his personal fortune into the temple treasury, prayed one of the most beautiful prayers in the Bible, and passed the crown to his son.

It was the last act of a king. And the Chronicler thought it was the most important thing David ever did.

SETTING THE KINGDOM IN ORDER

David was old. His life was drawing to a close, and he knew it. But instead of retiring to his palace and letting someone else worry about the future, he threw himself into one final project: making sure everything was ready for Solomon and the temple.

The organization described in chapters 23–27 is staggering in its detail. David divided the Levites into work groups and assigned their duties: maintaining the temple courts, preparing the bread for offerings, handling the flour and grain and baking, overseeing measurements and quantities, and standing every morning and evening to give thanks and praise to God.

He organized the priests into twenty-four divisions so they could rotate through the year, each family taking its turn serving at the altar. He arranged the musicians—288 trained singers and instrumentalists from the families of Asaph, Heman, and Jeduthun—into twenty-four groups, matching the priestly divisions. He appointed gatekeepers to guard the temple entrances, treasurers to protect the gold and silver and sacred objects stored inside, and judges to administer justice throughout the land.

He even organized his military into twelve divisions, one for each month, with commanders over each unit. He appointed tribal leaders, estate managers, and overseers for everything from the royal vineyards to the cattle herds to the olive groves.

If this sounds like a lot of administrative detail, that's because it is. And you might wonder why the Chronicler included all of it. After all, none of this appears in the books of Samuel or Kings. Why did the Chronicler think this mattered so much?

Because the Chronicler was writing for people who were rebuilding. His readers were the small community of returned exiles in Jerusalem, trying to restart temple worship from scratch. They needed to know that what they were doing—organizing priests and Levites, setting up worship schedules, assigning gatekeepers and singers—wasn't busywork. It was the very thing David had poured his final years into. If David thought it mattered enough to spend the last chapter of his life getting the details right, then the people rebuilding after the exile could know their work mattered too.

There's something else hidden in these chapters that's easy to miss. The musicians weren't just performers. The Chronicler says they were set apart "for the ministry of prophesying, accompanied by harps, lyres, and cymbals." The leaders of the three musical families—Asaph, Heman, and Jeduthun—are each called "seers" at various points in Chronicles. Their music wasn't entertainment. It was prophecy. When they sang, the Spirit of God was at work. Their songs carried the very word of God to the people.

And every role, from the highest-ranking musician to the person guarding the south gate, was assigned by lot, meaning God himself determined who served where. Young and old, experienced and inexperienced, major family and minor family, all received their assignments the same way. No favoritism. No pulling strings. God decided, and the people served where he placed them.

BLUEPRINTS FROM HEAVEN

Chapter 28 records one of the most dramatic scenes in David's life. He assembled all his leaders in Jerusalem—the tribal chiefs, military commanders, officials, and mighty warriors—stood to his feet, and gave his final public address.

David reminded them of his dream to build the temple and God's response: "You have shed much blood and fought many wars. You are not to build a house for my Name." Then he reminded them of God's promise: Solomon was chosen for the task. Solomon would sit on the throne of God's kingdom. Solomon would build the house.

But then David did something extraordinary. He handed Solomon the plans.

Not plans David had sketched on his own. The text says David gave his son "the plans of all that the Spirit had put in his mind." And later: "All this, in writing as a result of the Lord's hand on me, he enabled me to understand all the details of the plan."

Think about what that means. Just as God gave Moses the pattern for the tabernacle on Mount Sinai, God gave David the blueprint for the temple through his Spirit. Every detail— the portico, the storerooms, the inner rooms, the place of atonement, the golden lampstands and their exact weight, the silver tables, the gold forks and bowls, the altar of incense, and the golden chariot of the cherubim that would overshadow the ark—all of it came from God.

David wasn't just handing Solomon a construction project. He was handing him a window into heaven. The temple would be an earthly representation of God's heavenly throne. And God himself was the architect.

David's final words to Solomon echoed what God had said to Joshua centuries earlier: "Be strong and courageous, and do the work. Do not be afraid or discouraged, for the Lord God, my God, is with you. He will not fail you or forsake you until all the work for the service of the temple of the Lord is finished."

"WHO AM I?"

Then came chapter 29. And this is where the Chronicler's story of David reaches its peak—not in a battle, not in a conquest, but in an act of worship.

David stood before the assembly one more time and announced what he had given from his own personal treasury—not from the royal coffers, but from his own pocket—for the temple: gold, silver, bronze, iron, onyx, turquoise, stones of every color, fine stone, and marble, all in enormous quantities. "Because of my devotion to the house of my God," David said, "I now give my personal treasures of gold and silver for the temple of my God, over and above everything I have provided for this holy temple."

Then he looked at the assembly and asked a simple question: "Now, who is willing to consecrate themselves to the Lord today?"

The leaders responded. They gave five thousand talents of gold, ten thousand talents of silver, eighteen thousand talents of bronze, and a hundred thousand talents of iron, along with precious stones. The giving was massive. But what the Chronicler emphasizes isn't the amount. It's the spirit behind it: "The people rejoiced at the willing response of their leaders, for they had given freely and wholeheartedly to the Lord. David the king also rejoiced greatly."

That word "wholeheartedly" matters. It's one of the Chronicler's favorite ideas. Serving God with a whole heart—not half-hearted, not holding back, not calculating what you can afford to keep for yourself—is at the center of everything Chronicles teaches about faithfulness.

And then David prayed. This prayer, found only in Chronicles, is one of the great prayers of the Bible. It deserves to be read slowly.

"Yours, Lord, is the greatness and the power and the glory and the majesty and the splendor, for everything in heaven and earth is yours. Yours, Lord, is the kingdom; you are exalted as head over all."

David—the king, the empire-builder, the man who united the twelve tribes and defeated every enemy—looked at everything he had accomplished and said: it's all yours. The kingdom isn't mine. It's yours. The power isn't mine. It's yours. The glory? Yours.

Then came the line that captures everything: "But who am I, and who are my people, that we should be able to give as generously as this? Everything comes from you, and we have given you only what comes from your hand."

Read that again. Everything comes from you, and we have given you only what comes from your hand.

David had just given away a personal fortune. The leaders had poured out gold and silver by the ton. And David looked at all of it and said: we haven't really given you anything. It was all yours to begin with. We're just giving back what you gave us.

Then he said something even more striking: "We are foreigners and strangers in your sight, as were all our ancestors. Our days on earth are like a shadow, without hope."

This was the king of Israel. The man with the palace and the army and the dynasty that would last forever. And he called himself a foreigner and a stranger. His days were like a shadow. He held everything loosely because he understood that none of it was really his.

David prayed for his son: "Give my son Solomon the wholehearted devotion to keep your commands, statutes, and decrees, and to do everything to build the palatial structure for which I have provided."

Then the whole assembly blessed the Lord. They bowed down. They worshiped. They sacrificed thousands of burnt offerings. And they ate and drank with great joy in the presence of the Lord.

THE CROWN PASSES

Solomon was anointed king a second time—publicly, before all Israel—and he sat on the throne of the Lord as king in place of his father David. The text says something remarkable: Solomon didn't just sit on David's throne. He sat on "the throne of the Lord." The Chronicler wanted everyone to understand that this was God's kingdom, not David's and not Solomon's.

All the leaders and warriors pledged their loyalty. All of David's sons submitted to Solomon. The Lord exalted Solomon in the sight of all Israel and gave him royal splendor unlike any king before him.

And then David died. He had reigned forty years: seven at Hebron, thirty-three in Jerusalem. The Chronicler sums up his life in a single sentence: "He died at a good old age, having enjoyed long life, wealth, and honor." The story of David was over. But the story of God's kingdom was just getting started.

WHAT THIS MEANS FOR US

First, the details matter. David didn't just dream about the temple and leave someone else to figure out the logistics. He organized the priests, the musicians, the gatekeepers, the treasurers, and the judges. He worked out the rotations, the assignments, and the responsibilities. Faithfulness to God isn't just about the big, dramatic moments. It's about getting the details right in the small, unglamorous work that makes everything else possible.

Second, everything you have comes from God. David's prayer cuts through every illusion of self-sufficiency. Your abilities, your resources, your opportunities—none of it originated with you. Recognizing this doesn't make generosity harder. It makes it natural. If everything is a gift, then giving back to God isn't losing something. It's returning what was always his.

Third, wholehearted beats half-hearted every time. The word that echoes through these chapters is "wholeheartedly."

The leaders gave wholeheartedly. David urged Solomon to serve God with wholehearted devotion. The Chronicler cared less about the size of the gift than the condition of the heart behind it. God isn't impressed by going through the motions. He's looking for people who are all in.

Fourth, how you finish matters as much as how you start. David's final years weren't a slow fade into irrelevance. They were the most purposeful years of his life. He organized, prepared, gave, prayed, and passed the torch. The end of his story wasn't retirement. It was his greatest offering. How you finish—whether you stay faithful, stay generous, stay focused on God's purposes—says as much about your character as anything you did at the beginning.

TALKING POINTS

1. **David spent his final years organizing priests, musicians, gatekeepers, and judges for a temple he'd never see.** What does that tell you about what David valued most? How does this challenge the way we usually think about success and legacy?

2. **The temple blueprints came from God's Spirit, not from David's imagination.** Why is it significant that God was the architect of his own house? What does it tell us about how God wants to be worshiped—on his terms or ours?

3. **David prayed, "Everything comes from you, and we have given you only what comes from your hand."** How does this idea change the way you think about your own money, talents, and time? Is it harder or easier to be generous when you see everything as a gift?

4. David called himself a "foreigner and stranger" on the earth, even though he was the king of Israel. What did he mean? How should the awareness that our time on earth is temporary affect the way we live right now?

5. The people "rejoiced at the willing response of their leaders" and gave with great joy. Why do you think generosity and joy are so closely connected? When have you experienced joy in giving something away?

David's story ends where it should: on his knees, giving everything back to the God who gave it to him. The shepherd boy from Bethlehem became the greatest king Israel ever knew, but he never forgot where it all came from. He never forgot who he really was: a servant. A stranger passing through. A man whose only lasting treasure was the God he served.

Now it was Solomon's turn. He had the throne, the plans, the resources, the leaders, and the blessing of his father. Everything was in place.

The question was whether he would build with the same wholehearted devotion that David had shown, or whether he would settle for something less.

Turn the page.

<h1 style="text-align:center">5</h1>

WHEN GOD MOVED IN

Jonathan Swift's *Gulliver's Travels* takes its hero to some impossible places, but the most humbling might be Brobdingnag, the land of the giants. Everything there is enormous beyond imagination. The grass towers over Gulliver's head. A cat is the size of an ox. The king's palace sprawls like a city. And Gulliver himself? He's the size of an insect. The people hold him in the palm of their hand and peer down at him with amused curiosity. Everything Gulliver thought made him impressive—his learning, his speech, his accomplishments—suddenly means nothing. He's a tiny creature in a world too big for him to comprehend.

Solomon had a Gulliver moment.

He had just built the most magnificent building in the ancient world. The temple in Jerusalem was covered in gold—walls, ceiling, doors, even the nails. Cherubim with wings spanning the width of the inner sanctuary were overlaid with gold. The interior glowed like fire. Cedar from Lebanon. Purple and crimson fabric. Precious stones. A bronze altar so massive it dominated the courtyard. A circular basin called "the Sea," held up by twelve bronze oxen, large enough for the priests to wash in. Ten golden lampstands. Ten tables for sacred bread. A hundred gold bowls.

It was, by every measure, a masterpiece.

And then Solomon stood before the whole nation, looked at this dazzling structure, and said something that changed the meaning of everything he had built: "But will God really dwell on earth with humans? The heavens, even the highest heavens, cannot contain you. How much less this temple I have built!"

Solomon understood what Gulliver learned in Brobdingnag: no matter how impressive the thing you've made, it's nothing compared to the reality it's trying to hold. The temple was the greatest building on earth. But the God it was built for was bigger than the universe. The real question was never whether Solomon could build a house worthy of God. The answer to that would always be no. The real question was whether God would choose to show up anyway.

He did.

THE WISEST REQUEST

Second Chronicles opens with Solomon doing something his predecessor Saul never did: seeking God. Solomon gathered the entire nation at Gibeon, where the old tabernacle still stood, and offered a thousand burnt offerings on the bronze altar. That night, God appeared to him in a dream and asked a question that would test the new king's heart: "Ask for whatever you want me to give you."

Think about that. The Creator of the universe offering a blank check to a young king. Solomon could have asked for wealth, military power, long life, or the destruction of his enemies.

Instead, he asked for wisdom. "Give me wisdom and knowledge, that I may lead this people, for who is able to govern this great people of yours?"

God was pleased. Because Solomon hadn't asked for riches or honor or revenge, God gave him wisdom and knowledge, and then added wealth, possessions, and honor beyond anything any king before or after him would enjoy.

The Chronicler makes a point of this story that's easy to miss: Solomon *sought* God. That word appears more than forty times in Chronicles, far more than in Samuel or Kings. It's practically the Chronicler's theme song. Saul fell because he didn't seek God. David rose because he did. And now Solomon's reign begins on the right note because his first act as king was to seek the Lord.

For the Chronicler's audience, people trying to rebuild their lives after exile, this was a clear message: the starting point for everything is seeking God.

A TEMPLE THAT TOLD THE WORLD

Solomon's next move was to write a letter to Hiram, the king of Tyre, the powerful Phoenician trading city on the Mediterranean coast. Solomon needed cedar logs from the famous forests of Lebanon, and he needed skilled craftsmen who could work with gold, silver, bronze, and expensive fabrics. The Phoenicians were the best in the world at all of it.

But Solomon didn't just place an order. He made a declaration. In his letter to this foreign king, surrounded by his own foreign gods, Solomon wrote: "The temple I am going to build will be great, because our God is greater than all other gods."

That took nerve. Hiram worshiped his own deities. The Phoenicians had a whole pantheon of gods and goddesses. And here was Solomon telling their king that none of them compared to the Lord.

Hiram's response is one of the most surprising moments in Chronicles. Instead of being offended, he wrote back: "Praise be to the Lord, the God of Israel, who made heaven and earth!"

A pagan king praising the God of Israel. The Chronicler put this confession right at the beginning of the temple-building story on purpose. And he placed another one at the end, the queen of Sheba declaring, "Praise be to the Lord your God!" The entire temple narrative is framed by foreigners worshiping Israel's God. The temple wasn't just for Israel. It was meant to draw the nations to the Lord.

This is something the Chronicler emphasizes that the parallel account in 1 Kings doesn't highlight in the same way. The temple was an international project: built with Phoenician timber, shaped by a Phoenician craftsman named Huram-Abi, and intended to declare God's glory to every nation on earth.

A GARDEN MADE OF GOLD

When Solomon began building, the Chronicler notes the location with a detail that doesn't appear in 1 Kings: "Solomon began to build the temple of the Lord in Jerusalem on Mount Moriah, where the Lord had appeared to his father David. It was on the threshing floor of Araunah the Jebusite."

Mount Moriah. The same mountain where Abraham had nearly sacrificed Isaac. The same threshing floor where David had built an altar after the plague. Three of the most important moments in Israel's history—Abraham's test, David's repentance, Solomon's temple—all on the same hill. God was building on what he had started centuries before.

The temple itself was designed to echo something even older than Abraham. The golden cherubim in the inner sanctuary recalled the cherubim God placed at the entrance to the Garden of Eden after Adam and Eve were expelled. The palm trees and flowers carved into the walls and doors evoked a lush garden. The precious stones covering the interior reflected the jewels described in Eden. The "Sea," that enormous water basin, may have represented the rivers that flowed from Eden in the creation story.

The temple wasn't just a building. It was a miniature Eden. A place where God and his people could be together again, the way it was meant to be in the beginning. Everything that had been lost when sin entered the world—the closeness, the presence, the walking-with-God intimacy of the garden—was being restored, in part, in this sacred space.

THE MOMENT EVERYTHING CHANGED

When construction was complete, Solomon gathered all Israel for the dedication. The priests carried the ark of the covenant into the inner sanctuary and placed it beneath the wings of the golden cherubim. Inside the ark were the Ten Commandments, the physical evidence of God's covenant with his people.

Then something happened that only Chronicles describes in full detail. The Levitical musicians—all of them, from the families of Asaph, Heman, and Jeduthun—took their places on the east side of the altar, dressed in fine linen, playing cymbals, harps, and lyres. One hundred and twenty priests stood with them, holding trumpets. And then, all at once, as if with a single voice, the trumpeters and singers raised their instruments and their voices and sang in unison: "He is good; his love endures forever."

At that exact moment, while the music was still rising, while the words were still hanging in the air, a thick cloud filled the temple. The priests couldn't continue their service. They couldn't even stand. The glory of the Lord filled the house of God.

This was the moment the whole story had been building toward. Not the gold. Not the cedar. Not the craftsmanship. The glory. God himself, descending in a cloud just as he had descended on Mount Sinai, just as he had filled the tabernacle in the wilderness. The same God who walked with Adam in the garden was now dwelling in the temple Solomon had built.

God had moved in.

THE KING ON HIS KNEES

What happened next appears only in Chronicles: Solomon had built a bronze platform in the center of the outer court, five cubits long, five cubits wide, and three cubits high. In front of the entire assembly of Israel, the king climbed onto that platform, knelt down, and spread his hands toward heaven.

The most powerful man in the nation. On his knees. In public.

Solomon's prayer is one of the longest and most important in the Bible. He praised God for keeping his promise to David. He marveled that God would dwell on earth at all. And then he walked through seven different situations where God's people might need to cry out for help: when someone wrongs their neighbor, when Israel is defeated by enemies, when drought strikes, when famine or plague or disaster comes, when individuals are crushed by pain, when foreigners come seeking God, and when the nation goes to war.

In every single case, Solomon's request was the same: "Hear from heaven. Forgive."

One petition stands out. Solomon prayed for the foreigner, the person who didn't belong to Israel but who came from a distant land "because of your great name." Solomon asked God to do *whatever the foreigner asks*. Not "whatever your people ask"—whatever the *foreigner* asks. "So that all the peoples of the earth may know your name and fear you."

The temple was a house of prayer for all nations. Not just Israel. Everyone.

FIRE FROM HEAVEN

When Solomon finished praying, something happened that is recorded *only* in Chronicles. It doesn't appear in 1 Kings at all. Fire came down from heaven and consumed the burnt offerings and sacrifices. And the glory of the Lord filled the temple.

Fire from heaven. Just as fire had fallen on David's altar at the threshing floor. Just as fire had fallen from heaven on Mount Carmel when Elijah challenged the prophets of Baal. God answered Solomon's prayer the way he had answered before: with fire. Unmistakable. Undeniable. Visible to everyone.

The people fell facedown on the pavement, worshiping and giving thanks: "He is good; his love endures forever."

The celebration lasted fourteen days. Solomon offered twenty-two thousand cattle and a hundred and twenty thousand sheep. The Levites played their instruments. The priests served at their posts. And then, on the twenty-third day, Solomon sent the people home, "joyful and glad in heart for the good things the Lord had done."

THE PROMISE THAT ECHOES FOREVER

But God wasn't finished. After the people went home, the Lord appeared to Solomon at night with a personal message. He confirmed that he had heard Solomon's prayer. He had chosen this temple as a place for sacrifice. And then he spoke the words that would echo through the rest of Chronicles and into the hearts of God's people for thousands of years:

"If my people, who are called by my name, will humble themselves and pray and seek my face and turn from their wicked ways, then I will hear from heaven, and I will forgive their sin and will heal their land."

Four actions. One promise. Humble yourselves. Pray. Seek my face. Turn from wickedness. And God would hear, forgive, and heal.

For the Chronicler's audience—a small community that had experienced the devastation of exile, the destruction of this very temple, and decades of life in a foreign land—these words weren't ancient history. They were a lifeline. God was saying: the door is always open. No matter how far you've fallen, no matter how broken things are, the path back to me is the same as it's always been. Humble yourself. Pray. Seek me. Turn around. And I will heal what's broken.

Every king who comes after Solomon in Chronicles will be measured against this promise. The faithful ones—Asa, Jehoshaphat, Hezekiah, Josiah—will humble themselves and seek God, and they'll experience blessing. The unfaithful ones will refuse, and they'll experience the consequences. But the promise will stand, unchanged, all the way to the exile and beyond.

God keeps his word.

WHAT THIS MEANS FOR US

First, God wants to be found. The most remarkable thing about Chronicles isn't how great Solomon's temple was. It's that the God of the universe chose to show up in it. He didn't have to. The heavens can't contain him. But he wanted to dwell with his people. And he still does. God isn't hiding. He's inviting. The question isn't whether God is available. It's whether we're seeking him.

Second, the door is always open. The promise of 2 Chronicles 7:14 isn't complicated. It doesn't require special knowledge or impressive credentials. It requires humility, prayer, repentance, and seeking God. That's it. No matter what you've done or how far you've drifted, the way back is always the same.

Third, God's house is for everyone. Solomon prayed for foreigners. Hiram the Phoenician praised the Lord. The temple was designed to point the nations toward God. The gospel has always been for all people. God's invitation has never been limited to one group. If you've ever felt like you're on the outside looking in, the temple story says otherwise. God hears the foreigner's prayer too.

Fourth, worship is the appropriate response to God's presence. When the glory filled the temple, the people didn't applaud. They didn't analyze. They fell on their faces. When you encounter the living God—through his Word, through prayer, through the moments when his presence breaks through—the right response is worship. Not performance. Just awe.

TALKING POINTS

1. **Solomon asked for wisdom instead of wealth or power, and God gave him everything.** What does his choice reveal about what God values most? If God asked you, "What do you want?" how would you answer?

2. **Hiram, a foreign king, praised the God of Israel after hearing Solomon's declaration.** What does it take for people who don't share our faith to recognize the reality of God? How does the way we live and speak affect whether others are drawn to God?

3. **The temple was designed to echo the Garden of Eden: cherubim, garden imagery, precious stones.** What does it mean that God was creating a space where he could dwell with his people again? How does this connect to what Jesus accomplished?

4. **Fire fell from heaven when Solomon finished praying, a detail found only in Chronicles.** Why do you think the Chronicler included this? What does it reveal about how God responds to genuine worship and prayer?

5. **God's promise in 7:14 gives four steps: humble yourself, pray, seek God's face, and turn from wickedness.** Which of these four do you find most challenging, and why? How can you practice all four in your daily life?

The temple was built. The glory had descended. The promise had been given. For a brief, shining moment, everything was exactly as it should have been: God dwelling with his people, his presence filling the house, the nations taking notice.

But promises come with conditions. And the same God who promised to hear, forgive, and heal also warned Solomon what would happen if his people turned away. The story of what came next—a kingdom that split, kings who wandered, and a God who kept calling them back—was about to unfold.

Turn the page.

6

THE KINGDOM CRACKS

Disney's *The Little Mermaid* tells the story of a girl who has everything and throws it away for something she thinks she wants more. Ariel is a princess. She lives in a beautiful underwater kingdom. Her father is the most powerful king in the ocean. She has a voice that can fill the sea with music. But she becomes so obsessed with the world above the surface that she makes a terrible trade: she gives up her voice—the very thing that defines her—in exchange for a chance to walk on land. The deal nearly destroys her, her family, and her entire kingdom. The villain who brokered the deal almost wins. And the saddest part? Ariel had everything she needed. She just couldn't see it.

Something like that happens in 2 Chronicles 8–12. Solomon's kingdom was the most glorious in the world. Foreign kings brought tribute. A queen traveled fifteen hundred miles just to hear his wisdom. Gold was so plentiful in Jerusalem that silver was considered worthless. The temple shone like a beacon. The nations were taking notice of Israel's God. Solomon had everything.

And then it all cracked.

Not with a dramatic explosion. Not overnight. But steadily, quietly, the way a crack starts in a foundation: invisible at first, then spreading until the whole structure splits. By the end of these chapters, the kingdom that David built and Solomon adorned will be torn in two, its treasures plundered, and its glory reduced to bronze replicas of what used to be gold.

The story of how it happened, and what the Chronicler wants us to learn from it, is one of the most important sections in all of Chronicles.

THE PEAK

Before the fall came the summit. Second Chronicles 8–9 describe Solomon's kingdom at its absolute height. He built cities throughout the land. He fortified strategic locations along trade routes. He launched maritime expeditions to a distant land called Ophir, where his ships returned laden with 450 talents of gold. He accumulated horses and chariots from Egypt, cedar from Lebanon, and exotic goods from across the known world. Silver and gold were so abundant in Jerusalem that the text says silver "was considered of little value."

And then came the queen of Sheba.

She had heard about Solomon from fifteen hundred miles away in what is now Yemen, at the southern tip of the Arabian Peninsula. She didn't just send a messenger. She came herself, with a massive caravan of camels carrying spices, gold, and precious stones. She came to test Solomon with hard questions, and he answered every one of them. When she saw his wisdom, his palace, the food on his table, the robes of his servants, the offerings he made at the temple, the text says "she was overwhelmed."

Then she spoke words that the Chronicler placed here with surgical precision: "Praise be to the Lord your God, who has delighted in you and placed you on his throne as king to rule for the Lord your God."

Did you catch the detail the Chronicler changed? In 1 Kings, the queen says Solomon sits on "the throne of Israel." In Chronicles, she says he sits on God's throne, ruling for God. The Chronicler wanted everyone to understand: this kingdom belongs to God, not Solomon. The king is a steward, not an owner.

And remember: this is a *foreigner* praising the Lord. Earlier, King Hiram of Tyre opened the temple narrative by declaring, "Praise be to the Lord, the God of Israel, who made heaven and earth!" Now the queen of Sheba closes it with her own confession of praise. The Chronicler has framed the entire story of the temple—its building, dedication, and glory—between two declarations by outsiders who recognized Israel's God. The temple wasn't just for Israel. Its purpose was to draw the nations to the Lord.

For the small, struggling community that read Chronicles after the exile, this was a vision worth holding onto. The nations had once come to Jerusalem. They could come again. God's plan to reach the world through his people was still in play.

WHAT THE CHRONICLER DIDN'T SAY

Here's something remarkable. If you read 1 Kings 11, you'll find one of the most devastating chapters in the Old Testament. Solomon, the wisest man who ever lived, married hundreds of foreign women who turned his heart toward other gods. He built shrines to Ashtoreth, Chemosh, and Molech, the same gods whose worship included child sacrifice. God told Solomon directly that the kingdom would be torn from his son because of his unfaithfulness.

The Chronicler doesn't tell that story. He skips it entirely.

Why? Not because he didn't know about it. Everyone knew. The Chronicler even mentions the prophet Ahijah, whose prophecy to Jeroboam is the hinge on which the whole kingdom-split story turns. The readers would have filled in the blanks.

The Chronicler left it out because his focus was different. He wasn't writing a biography of Solomon. He was writing a theology of hope. His message to the post-exilic community wasn't "look how badly Solomon failed" but "look how God kept working despite Solomon's failure." Even after the worst idolatry imaginable, God didn't abandon his plan. He didn't abandon his people. He adjusted the consequences but kept moving forward.

That said, the Chronicler drops quiet hints. He notes that Solomon accumulated horses, wives, and gold, the three things Moses, in Deuteronomy, explicitly told kings *not* to accumulate. He records that Pharaoh's daughter had to live in a separate palace because she couldn't be near the ark. And the final summary of Solomon's reign includes no statement about his heart being devoted to God, a conspicuous silence compared to what the Chronicler says about faithful kings like Hezekiah and Josiah.

The glory was real. But something underneath had gone wrong. And what was broken in private was about to become devastatingly public.

THE WORST DECISION IN ISRAEL'S HISTORY

When Solomon died, his son Rehoboam traveled to Shechem to be crowned king. All Israel gathered there, including a man named Jeroboam, who had fled to Egypt during Solomon's reign after a prophet told him God would give him ten of the twelve tribes.

The people had one request: "Your father put a heavy yoke on us. Lighten the harsh labor and we will serve you."

It was a reasonable ask. Solomon's building projects had been magnificent, but the cost in human labor had been enormous. The people were exhausted.

Rehoboam asked his father's experienced advisors what to do. Their counsel was wise: be kind, give the people a favorable answer, and they'll serve you forever.

Then Rehoboam did something catastrophic. He ignored the elders and went to his young friends instead. Their advice dripped with arrogance: "Tell them your little finger is thicker than your father's waist. Tell them you'll make things *worse*."

Rehoboam listened to his friends. Three days later, he delivered the most foolish speech a king of Israel ever made: "My father made your yoke heavy; I will make it even heavier. My father scourged you with whips; I will scourge you with scorpions."

The northern tribes walked out. Ten tribes declared independence. The united kingdom of David and Solomon, the kingdom God had spent generations building, shattered in a single afternoon.

The Chronicler adds a note that might surprise you: "This turn of events was from God, to fulfill the word the Lord had spoken to Jeroboam through Ahijah the Shilonite." God was behind this. Not because he wanted the kingdom to split, but because Solomon's unfaithfulness had consequences that couldn't be erased by a change of leadership. The crack in the foundation had already formed. Rehoboam's arrogance just made it visible.

THE FAITHFUL WHO WALKED SOUTH

What happened next is found only in Chronicles. It's one of the most important passages in the book, and you won't find it in 1 Kings.

Jeroboam, now king of the northern tribes, knew he had a problem. If his people kept traveling to Jerusalem to worship at the temple, their loyalty might eventually drift back to the house of David. So he set up two golden calves—one in Dan and one in Bethel—and told the people, "Here are your gods, Israel, who brought you up out of Egypt." He appointed his own priests from outside the tribe of Levi and established his own religious festivals.

The echoes of the golden calf at Sinai were unmistakable. Israel had made this mistake before.

But here's what the Chronicler records that Kings doesn't: "The priests and Levites from all their districts throughout Israel sided with [Rehoboam]. The Levites even abandoned their pasturelands and property and came to Judah and Jerusalem, because Jeroboam and his sons had rejected them as priests of the Lord."

The Levites walked away from everything they owned. They left their homes, their land, their livelihoods, and moved south to Judah because they refused to participate in false worship. And they weren't alone: "Those from every tribe of Israel who set their hearts on seeking the Lord, the God of Israel, followed the Levites to Jerusalem."

From *every* tribe. People who loved God more than comfort, more than property, more than tribal loyalty, packed up and moved. They strengthened Rehoboam's kingdom for three years.

For the Chronicler's audience, this was electric. It meant the southern kingdom, the community they descended from, had always included faithful people from the north. The "all Israel" ideal wasn't dead. It had been kept alive by people who chose God over convenience. And if it had happened before, it could happen again.

WHEN STRENGTH BECAME A TRAP

For three years, Rehoboam walked in the ways of David and Solomon. Things were stable. The kingdom was growing stronger.

Then the Chronicler delivers one of the most chilling sentences in the book: "After Rehoboam's position as king was established and he had become strong, he and all Israel with him abandoned the law of the Lord."

Strength became a trap. When things were going well, when the kingdom felt secure, when Rehoboam felt he didn't need God anymore, he walked away. The same pattern that brought down Solomon was now repeating in his son.

The consequence was swift. Shishak, pharaoh of Egypt, invaded Judah with twelve hundred chariots, sixty thousand horsemen, and troops beyond counting. He captured the fortified cities Rehoboam had built and marched all the way to Jerusalem.

Then a prophet named Shemaiah arrived with a message that captured the entire theology of Chronicles in a single sentence: "You have abandoned me; therefore, I now abandon you to Shishak."

You abandoned me. I abandon you. The symmetry was devastating. It was the flip side of the promise God had made to Solomon: "If my people will humble themselves and pray and seek my face and turn from their wicked ways, then I will hear from heaven." The promise works both directions. Seek God, and he is found. Abandon God, and the protection lifts.

THE TURN

But the story didn't end there. When Rehoboam and the leaders heard the prophet's words, they did something the Chronicler had been waiting to record: "They humbled themselves."

Three words. But those three words changed everything.

"When the Lord saw that they humbled themselves, this word of the Lord came to Shemaiah: 'Since they have humbled themselves, I will not destroy them but will soon give them deliverance. My wrath will not be poured out on Jerusalem through Shishak.'"

God relented. Not because Rehoboam deserved it. Not because the people had earned it. But because they humbled themselves. That's the pattern the Chronicler is teaching, and it will repeat again and again through the rest of the book: pride leads to disaster, but humility opens the door to mercy.

The consequences weren't erased entirely. Shishak still plundered the temple and the palace. He carried off the gold shields Solomon had made—those gleaming symbols of Israel's glory—and Rehoboam replaced them with bronze. Gold to bronze. That image says everything about what happens when a kingdom turns away from God. You don't lose everything all at once. You lose the gold and replace it with something cheaper, and eventually you forget what the original looked like.

But Jerusalem survived. The temple stood. And the Chronicler offered this quiet verdict: "Because Rehoboam humbled himself, the Lord's anger turned from him, and he was not totally destroyed. Indeed, there was some good in Judah."

Some good. Not a ringing endorsement. But enough. God found enough to work with. He always does.

WHAT THIS MEANS FOR US

First, success without God is a trap. Solomon had everything, and it wasn't enough. Rehoboam grew strong and abandoned God. The pattern repeats throughout history: when things go well, we forget who made them go well. The most dangerous moments in your spiritual life aren't the hard times. They're the easy times: when you feel strong, when things are working, when you stop feeling like you need God.

Second, arrogance breaks what wisdom builds. David built a united kingdom through decades of seeking God. Solomon expanded it through wisdom. Rehoboam destroyed it in a single conversation because he was too proud to listen to wise counsel. One arrogant decision can undo years of faithful work. Humility isn't weakness. It's the thing that holds everything together.

Third, God always preserves a faithful remnant. When the north collapsed into idolatry, the Levites and the seekers of

God walked south. They left everything behind because worship of the true God mattered more than comfort. In every generation, no matter how dark things get, God has people who refuse to compromise. You can be one of them.

Fourth, humility changes God's response. Rehoboam deserved destruction. He got mercy because he humbled himself. That's the promise of 2 Chronicles 7:14 in action. God doesn't demand perfection. He demands honesty. When you stop pretending, stop posturing, and simply admit that you need him, God responds with grace.

TALKING POINTS

1. **The queen of Sheba was a foreigner who praised God after seeing Solomon's kingdom.** What does it tell you about God's plan that the temple narrative is framed by two foreigners worshiping the Lord? How should this shape how we think about people outside our faith community?

2. **Rehoboam ignored wise counsel from experienced elders and listened to arrogant friends instead.** Why is it so tempting to listen to people who tell us what we want to hear? How can you tell the difference between wise advice and foolish advice?

3. **The Levites left their homes and property in the north because they refused to participate in false worship.** What would it take for you to give up something comfortable for the sake of following God? Have you ever had to make a hard choice between convenience and faithfulness?

4. **The Chronicler says Rehoboam abandoned God after he "became strong."** Why does strength or success sometimes

lead people away from God instead of closer to him? How can we stay humble when things are going well?

5. **When Rehoboam humbled himself, God showed mercy, but the gold shields were still replaced with bronze.** What does this teach us about the relationship between forgiveness and consequences? Can God forgive us and still allow us to experience the results of our choices?

The kingdom was divided. The gold was gone. The glory had dimmed. But God wasn't finished. What followed was a long line of kings—some faithful, some disastrous—and with each one, the Chronicler would ask the same question: Did this king seek God, or did he abandon him? The answer determined everything.

Turn the page.

7

TWO KINDS OF KINGS

Miguel de Cervantes' *Don Quixote* tells the story of a man who does things nobody understands. He charges at windmills with a lance, convinced they're giants. He attacks a flock of sheep, thinking they're an enemy army. He wears a basin on his head and calls it a helmet. Everyone around him—his squire, his neighbors, the people he meets on the road—thinks he's out of his mind. And honestly? Most of the time, he is.

But there's one thing Don Quixote gets right that everyone else gets wrong: he believes the world is bigger than what you can see. He believes invisible forces are at work. He believes that sometimes the bravest thing you can do is act on what you believe even when everyone else thinks you're crazy.

Hold that thought. Because in 2 Chronicles 20, a king named Jehoshaphat does something that would have made Don Quixote proud. Facing the largest enemy army he's ever seen—a coalition of nations marching on Jerusalem—Jehoshaphat doesn't send his best soldiers to the front. He sends the choir.

Singers. In robes. With no weapons. Marching ahead of the army, singing at the top of their lungs: "Give thanks to the Lord, for his love endures forever."

And it worked.

That story is the crown jewel of a section of Chronicles that covers twelve chapters, a dozen kings, and one relentless question the Chronicler asks about every single one of them: Did this king seek God, or didn't he? The answer determined everything.

THE PATTERN

Second Chronicles 13–24 covers roughly 150 years of the southern kingdom of Judah. Kings come and go. Some reign for decades, others for a single year. Some are faithful; others are disasters. But underneath all the individual stories, the Chronicler is tracing a pattern that he wants his readers to see clearly, the same pattern God laid out in 2 Chronicles 7:14.

Seek God, and he will be found by you. Forsake him, and he will forsake you. Humble yourself, and he will deliver you. Refuse to humble yourself, and consequences will follow.

The Chronicler doesn't hide this pattern. He puts it right on the surface, sometimes in the mouths of prophets who show up at exactly the right moment with exactly the right message. Almost all of these prophetic speeches are unique to Chronicles; you won't find them in 1–2 Kings. The Chronicler added them because he wanted his post-exilic readers to understand that the principles hadn't changed. What was true for Asa and Jehoshaphat was true for them. It's true for us.

THE KING WHO PRAYED AGAINST AN ARMY

Asa was one of the good ones. He tore down the foreign altars and pagan shrines. He commanded Judah to seek the Lord and follow his laws. The land had peace for ten years under his leadership.

Then a massive army appeared.

A commander named Zerah led a Cushite force from the south, thousands upon thousands of soldiers with hundreds of chariots. Asa's army was badly outnumbered. By every military calculation, Judah should have been crushed.

This battle is found only in Chronicles. It doesn't appear in 1 Kings. And the Chronicler included it because of what Asa did next.

Instead of panicking or calculating the odds, Asa prayed: "Lord, there is no one like you to help the powerless against the mighty. Help us, Lord our God, for we rely on you, and in your name we have come against this vast army. Lord, you are our God; do not let mere mortals prevail against you."

Notice what Asa didn't say. He didn't say, "We've got a great strategy." He didn't say, "Our soldiers are well-trained." He said, "We are powerless. We rely on you." He admitted weakness. He acknowledged dependence. He put everything on God.

God struck down the Cushites. Asa's army won a victory that should have been impossible. The Chronicler's point wasn't subtle: when God's people are honest about their weakness and cry out to him, he fights for them.

THE PROPHET'S WARNING

After the victory, a prophet named Azariah met Asa with a message that became one of the defining statements of the entire book. This speech exists only in Chronicles:

"The Lord is with you when you are with him. If you seek him, he will be found by you, but if you forsake him, he will forsake you."

Then Azariah reminded Asa of Israel's history during the time of the judges, a time when the nation had no true God, no priest to teach, and no law. The result? Chaos. Violence. One nation crushed by another. Nobody was safe.

Three essentials of faith, the prophet said. The true God. Teachers of his word. And the law itself. Take any of those away, and everything falls apart.

Asa listened. He removed the remaining idols. He repaired the altar. He gathered the people for a covenant renewal, and they swore to seek the Lord with all their heart. People even came from the northern tribes because they saw that God was with Asa.

The tragedy of Asa's story is that it didn't end there. In his later years, when a different enemy threatened, Asa didn't pray. He made a political alliance with a foreign king instead, buying help with gold from the temple. A prophet confronted him: "Because you relied on the king of Aram and not on the Lord your God, the army of the king of Aram has escaped from your hand." Asa had relied on God when he was weak, but when he felt strong, he relied on himself. It cost him.

The Chronicler's warning was clear: past faithfulness doesn't guarantee future obedience. You have to keep seeking.

THE KING WHO SENT TEACHERS

Asa's son Jehoshaphat was, in many ways, the Chronicler's model king. He sought God early in his reign. He removed the high places and idols. He strengthened the kingdom. But the detail the Chronicler highlights most is this: Jehoshaphat sent officials, Levites, and priests to travel through every city in Judah, carrying the Book of the Law with them, teaching God's word to the people.

This wasn't a one-time revival meeting. It was a systematic, kingdom-wide program of Scripture education. The Chronicler cared deeply about this because his own community, the post-exilic remnant, was in danger of losing its connection to God's word. The prophet Azariah had warned what happens when there's no priest to teach and no law. Jehoshaphat made sure that wouldn't happen on his watch.

The result? The fear of the Lord fell on the surrounding nations. Not because Jehoshaphat had a bigger army, but because God was with him. Even the Philistines and Arabians brought tribute. The kingdom flourished, not through military might but through devotion to God and his word.

THE BATTLE WON BY SINGING

Then came the crisis that produced the most unforgettable scene in all of Chronicles. A coalition of Moabites, Ammonites, and Meunites marched on Judah. The army was vast. They had already reached En Gedi, only thirty-five miles from Jerusalem. There was no time to recruit allies or develop a strategy.

Jehoshaphat was terrified. But instead of calling his generals, he called a fast. He gathered all of Judah—men, women, and children—to seek the Lord together. Then he stood in the temple courtyard and prayed a prayer that every person who has ever faced an impossible situation should memorize:

"Our God, will you not judge them? For we have no power to face this vast army that is attacking us. We do not know what to do, but our eyes are on you."

We do not know what to do, but our eyes are on you. That's it. That's the prayer. No strategy. No solution. Just honest desperation and total trust.

Then God answered. His Spirit fell on a Levite named Jahaziel, who declared: "Do not be afraid or discouraged because of this vast army. For the battle is not yours, but God's. You will not have to fight this battle. Take up your positions; stand firm and see the deliverance the Lord will give you."

The next morning, Jehoshaphat made the most outrageous military decision in Israel's history. He appointed singers to march at the front of the army—ahead of the soldiers, ahead of the shields and spears—singing, "Give thanks to the Lord, for his love endures forever."

As they began to sing and praise, God set ambushes against the invading armies. The Ammonites and Moabites turned on the men from Mount Seir and destroyed them. Then they turned on each other. By the time Judah arrived at the overlook, there was no army left to fight. Only dead bodies and plunder—so much plunder that it took three days to collect it all.

They named the place the Valley of Blessing.

This entire story is unique to Chronicles. The Chronicler included it because it demonstrated everything he wanted his readers to understand: the battle belongs to God. Your weakness isn't disqualifying; it's the starting point. And worship isn't something you do after you win. It's the weapon that wins the fight.

THE DARK YEARS

Not every king followed the pattern. After Jehoshaphat died, the kingdom spiraled into its darkest period.

Jehoshaphat's son Jehoram married Athaliah, the daughter of the wicked northern king Ahab. Under her influence, Jehoram murdered his own brothers, led Judah into Baal worship, and received a devastating letter from the prophet Elijah (a detail found only in Chronicles) warning him that God would strike his people, his sons, his wives, and everything he had.

When Jehoram's son Ahaziah was killed, Athaliah herself seized the throne and massacred the entire royal family. Every descendant of David. The line that God had promised would last forever was being slaughtered by a single power-hungry woman.

But one baby survived. Jehosheba, the king's daughter and wife of the priest Jehoiada, smuggled the infant Joash out of the palace and hid him in the temple for six years. One child. One priest. One brave woman. That's all that stood between God's promise and total destruction.

When Joash turned seven, Jehoiada organized a coup. He brought the boy out, crowned him king, and the people shouted, "Long live the king!" Athaliah was executed. The temple of Baal was torn down. For as long as Jehoiada the priest lived, Joash did what was right.

But after Jehoiada died—the man who had saved Joash's life, who had mentored him, who had guided his every decision—the king listened to different voices. Officials who wanted to worship other gods. Joash abandoned the temple his mentor had helped him restore and turned to idols. When

Jehoiada's own son Zechariah stood up and warned the king, Joash had him stoned to death in the temple courtyard.

The man who owed everything to the priest's family killed the priest's son. It's one of the most tragic reversals in the Bible.

WHAT THIS MEANS FOR US

First, admitting weakness is the beginning of strength. Asa said, "We are powerless." Jehoshaphat said, "We do not know what to do." Neither statement was a failure of leadership. Both were acts of faith. The world tells you to project confidence and hide your struggles. God says the opposite: bring me your weakness, and I'll show you my strength.

Second, knowing God's word is not optional. Jehoshaphat didn't just tell people to seek God. He sent teachers to every city with the Book of the Law. The prophet Azariah warned that a nation without teachers and without the law collapses into chaos. Faith that isn't grounded in Scripture doesn't survive. If you want to seek God, start with his word.

Third, worship is more powerful than you think. Jehoshaphat sent singers ahead of the army, and God won the battle. That doesn't mean you should stop studying for tests and just sing worship songs instead. But it does mean that when you face something bigger than you can handle, praise is a legitimate response, not because you're pretending things are fine, but because you're declaring that God is bigger than the problem.

Fourth, influence matters more than you realize. Joash was faithful as long as Jehoiada was alive. The moment his mentor died, he caved to pressure from people who didn't love God.

The people around you shape who you become. Choose your influences carefully, because the voices you listen to after your "Jehoiada" is gone will determine the direction of your life.

TALKING POINTS

1. **Asa prayed, "Do not let mere mortals prevail against you."** Why did he frame the battle as an attack against God rather than against Israel? How does seeing your struggles as God's battles (not just your own) change the way you respond to them?

2. **The prophet Azariah said Israel's worst times came when they had "no true God, no priest to teach, and no law."** Which of those three do you think is most lacking in the world today? What role does teaching and learning play in keeping faith alive?

3. **Jehoshaphat's first response to the enemy army was to call a fast and gather the people to pray, not to call his generals.** What does this say about what should come first when you face a crisis? Is prayer usually your first response or your last resort?

4. **Jehoshaphat sent the choir ahead of the army.** What would it look like in your own life to "lead with worship" when facing something scary or overwhelming? How is this different from pretending the problem doesn't exist?

5. **Joash was faithful while Jehoiada was alive but turned away after the priest died.** What does this tell you about the danger of depending on someone else's faith instead of developing your own? How can you build a faith that lasts even when your mentors are no longer around?

The pattern was set. Seek God, and he answers. Forsake him, and the consequences come. Humble yourself, and the door to mercy swings open. Every king who came to the throne faced the same choice. The next group of kings would prove that the pattern still held, for better and for worse.

Turn the page.

8

THE END THAT WASN'T

There's a moment near the end of Disney's *Beauty and the Beast* when everything seems lost. The last petal is about to fall from the enchanted rose. The Beast lies dying on the balcony, rain pouring down on the stone. The servants have frozen into lifeless objects—a clock that no longer ticks, a candelabra that no longer flickers. The castle, already crumbling for years, feels like a tomb. Belle is there, but she's too late. She whispers, "I love you," and the final petal drops.

It's over. The curse has won. There is no time left.

And then light begins to fall from the sky. The Beast rises. The curse shatters. The gargoyles crack open and reveal angels. The servants come back to life. The entire castle transforms—every broken stone, every shattered window, every darkened hallway floods with light and color. What looked like the end was actually the moment everything changed.

The last twelve chapters of 2 Chronicles tell a story like that. The kingdom of Judah spirals downward through a succession of kings—some faithful, most not—until finally the Babylonians burn Jerusalem, destroy the temple, and drag the survivors into exile. It looks like the end. The promise to David seems dead. The covenant seems broken beyond repair.

And then, in the final two verses of the entire book, something impossible happens. A Persian emperor named Cyrus, a foreigner who didn't worship Israel's God, issues a decree: "The Lord, the God of heaven, has given me all the kingdoms of the earth and he has appointed me to build a temple for him at Jerusalem in Judah. Any of his people among you may go up, and may the Lord their God be with them."

The end wasn't the end. It was the beginning of something new.

THE KING WHO REACHED TOO FAR

The downward spiral had warning signs along the way. King Uzziah, one of the longest-reigning kings in Judah's history, was one of them.

Uzziah did almost everything right. He sought God during the early years of his reign. He built up the kingdom's military, fortified cities, and expanded the territory. He was an innovator. The Chronicler notes his interest in agriculture and his construction of defensive towers. As long as he sought the Lord, God gave him success.

Then came the sentence the Chronicler uses like a warning siren: "But after Uzziah became powerful, his pride led to his downfall."

Uzziah walked into the temple, the holy place reserved exclusively for priests, and picked up a censer to burn incense on the golden altar. Eighty priests confronted him: "It is not right for you, Uzziah, to burn incense to the Lord. That is for the priests, the descendants of Aaron, who have been consecrated to burn incense. Leave the sanctuary, for you have been unfaithful."

Uzziah didn't repent. He raged at them. And while he was still shouting, standing by the incense altar with the censer in his hand, leprosy broke out on his forehead. The priests rushed him out. He spent the rest of his life in a separate house, cut off from the temple he had violated. His son Jotham governed in his place.

The Chronicler's account of Uzziah's leprosy is far more detailed than what appears in Kings. He included it because it illustrated a principle his readers needed to understand: power without humility leads to destruction. The same God who gives success can take it away when pride takes root.

THE ENEMIES WHO SHOWED MERCY

The low point before the lowest point came during the reign of Ahaz, one of Judah's worst kings. Ahaz worshiped foreign gods, sacrificed his own children in fire, and shut the doors of the temple. Under his leadership, Judah became indistinguishable from the pagan nations God had driven out of the land centuries earlier.

God allowed enemies to invade. The northern kingdom of Israel attacked Judah and carried away thousands of captives along with enormous plunder.

Then something happened that exists only in Chronicles. A prophet named Oded met the northern army as they returned to Samaria with their captives. He told them bluntly: you won because God was angry at Judah, not because you're righteous. And now you intend to enslave your own brothers and sisters? "Do you not also have sins of your own against the Lord your God?"

Leaders from the tribe of Ephraim backed up the prophet. They refused to let the captives be enslaved. And then—in one of the most surprising scenes in all of Chronicles—those northern soldiers, the ones who had just invaded Judah, clothed the prisoners, gave them sandals, fed them, gave them something to drink, anointed their wounds, put the weak ones on donkeys, and personally escorted them back to Jericho.

If that sounds like the parable of the Good Samaritan, it should. This story, set in the territory of Samaria, involving people who showed unexpected compassion to their enemies, may well have been in Jesus' mind centuries later when he told his famous parable about a Samaritan who stopped to help a wounded stranger. Even in one of the darkest chapters of Judah's history, God's mercy showed up through the last people anyone expected.

THE KING WHO OPENED THE DOORS

After Ahaz died, his son Hezekiah became king and did something stunning: in the first month of the first year of his reign, before doing anything else, he opened the doors of the temple that his father had shut.

What follows is one of the longest and most detailed sections in all of Chronicles: four full chapters devoted to Hezekiah's reign. And almost none of it appears in 2 Kings. The Chronicler gave Hezekiah more attention than any king since Solomon because Hezekiah embodied everything the Chronicler wanted his post-exilic readers to become.

Hezekiah gathered the priests and Levites and told them to consecrate themselves and purify the temple. "Our parents were unfaithful," he said. "They did evil in the eyes of the Lord our God and forsook him." The cleansing took sixteen days. Every unclean object was hauled out and dumped in the Kidron Valley. The sacred furniture that Ahaz had discarded was retrieved, repaired, and returned to its place. Then the sacrifices resumed, the Levites played their instruments, and worship began again.

But Hezekiah wasn't finished. He did something no king since Solomon had done: he invited the northern tribes to come to Jerusalem and celebrate the Passover.

He sent couriers throughout Ephraim and Manasseh, territories that had broken away two hundred years earlier, with letters that said: "People of Israel, return to the Lord, the God of Abraham, Isaac, and Israel, that he may return to you who are left, who have escaped from the hand of the kings of Assyria."

Most people in the north laughed. They scorned the messengers and ridiculed the invitation. But some from Asher, Manasseh, and Zebulun humbled themselves and came to Jerusalem. People from Ephraim, Manasseh, Issachar, and Zebulun joined Judah for the Passover, the first time in centuries that representatives of the northern and southern tribes worshiped together in Jerusalem.

Many of the northerners hadn't properly consecrated themselves according to the law. They shouldn't have been allowed to eat the Passover. But Hezekiah prayed for them: "May the Lord, who is good, pardon everyone who sets their heart on seeking God—the Lord, the God of their ancestors—even if they are not clean according to the rules of the sanctuary." And God heard Hezekiah and healed the people.

Grace made room for everyone who came with a seeking heart.

The celebration was so joyful that they extended it an extra seven days. The Chronicler recorded that "there was great joy in Jerusalem, for since the days of Solomon son of David king of Israel there had been nothing like this in Jerusalem."

For one shining moment, it looked like the Chronicler's dream of a reunited Israel was coming true.

THE WORST KING WHO FOUND MERCY

Then came Manasseh. And everything fell apart again.

Manasseh was the worst king in Judah's history. The Chronicler's list of his sins reads like a catalog of horrors: he rebuilt the high places his father Hezekiah had destroyed. He erected altars to foreign gods in the temple itself. He practiced sorcery, divination, and witchcraft. He sacrificed his own sons in the fire. He set up a carved idol in God's house. The text says he "led Judah and the people of Jerusalem astray, so that they did more evil than the nations the Lord had destroyed before the Israelites."

If you read 2 Kings, that's where Manasseh's story ends: in unrelieved darkness. Kings records his sins and moves on.

But Chronicles tells us something Kings doesn't. And it's the most shocking twist in the entire book.

"The Lord brought against them the army commanders of the king of Assyria, who took Manasseh prisoner, put a hook in his nose, bound him with bronze shackles and took him to Babylon. In his distress he sought the favor of the Lord his God and humbled himself greatly before the God of his ancestors. And when he prayed to him, the Lord was moved by his entreaty and listened to his plea; so he brought him back to Jerusalem and to his kingdom. Then Manasseh knew that the Lord is God."

Read that again. The worst king. The one who filled Jerusalem with innocent blood. The one who put idols in God's own temple. Dragged away in chains, a hook in his nose. And in that moment of total humiliation, he did the one thing he had never done: he humbled himself and prayed.

And God heard him.

God didn't just hear him. God *restored* him. Brought him back to Jerusalem. Gave him his kingdom again. And Manasseh—the man nobody would have expected to reform—removed the foreign gods, took the idol out of the temple, rebuilt the altar of the Lord, and offered sacrifices of thanksgiving.

This story exists only in Chronicles. The Chronicler included it because it was the ultimate proof of the promise God made to Solomon: "If my people, who are called by my name, will humble themselves and pray and seek my face and turn from their wicked ways, then I will hear from heaven, and I will forgive their sin and will heal their land."

If God could forgive Manasseh, he could forgive anyone. If Manasseh could find his way back, nobody was beyond hope.

The Chronicler even contrasted Manasseh with his son Amon, who committed the same sins but, unlike his father, "did not humble himself before the Lord." Same sins. Different response. Humility made the difference.

THE LAST GOOD KING AND THE FINAL FALL

Josiah was the last bright spot. He became king at age eight and began seeking God at sixteen. He purged the land of idols and high places. When workers discovered the lost Book of the Law during temple repairs, Josiah tore his robes and wept because he realized how far the nation had drifted from God's commands. He celebrated a Passover so meticulous in its observance of the law that the Chronicler said nothing like it had been held since the days of Samuel.

But even Josiah's faithfulness couldn't undo what was coming. He died in a battle he shouldn't have fought against an Egyptian pharaoh who actually warned him that God had sent him and that Josiah shouldn't interfere. Josiah didn't listen. It cost him his life.

After Josiah, the kingdom collapsed in rapid succession. His sons and grandsons ruled briefly and badly. Jehoahaz lasted three months. Jehoiakim lasted eleven years but "did evil in the eyes of the Lord." Jehoiachin lasted three months. And finally Zedekiah, the last king, who "did evil in the eyes of the Lord his God and did not humble himself before Jeremiah the prophet, who spoke the word of the Lord."

The Chronicler paused here to deliver his final theological verdict on why the exile happened: "The Lord, the God of their ancestors, sent word to them through his messengers again and again, because he had pity on his people and on his dwelling place. But they mocked God's messengers, despised his words, and scoffed at his prophets until the wrath of the Lord was aroused against his people and there was no remedy."

No remedy. The most devastating two-word phrase in the book. God had been patient, sending prophets "again and again." But his people had mocked, despised, and scoffed until there was nothing left to do.

Nebuchadnezzar came. He killed young and old in the sanctuary itself. He burned the temple. He tore down Jerusalem's walls. He carried the survivors to Babylon. The sacred vessels that Solomon had crafted were hauled away as trophies.

"The land enjoyed its sabbath rests," the Chronicler wrote with bitter irony. The land that Israel had refused to let rest—the sabbath years they had skipped—now got its rest by force, "until the seventy years were completed in fulfillment of the word of the Lord spoken by Jeremiah."

TWO VERSES THAT CHANGED EVERYTHING

If the book ended there, it would be the darkest ending in the Bible.

But it doesn't end there.

"In the first year of Cyrus king of Persia, in order to fulfill the word of the Lord spoken by Jeremiah, the Lord moved the heart of Cyrus king of Persia to make a proclamation throughout his realm and also to put it in writing: 'This is what Cyrus king of Persia says: The Lord, the God of heaven, has given me all the kingdoms of the earth and he has appointed me to build a temple for him at Jerusalem in Judah. Any of his people among you may go up, and may the Lord their God be with them.'"

Those are the last words of 2 Chronicles. The entire book—sixty-five chapters, from Adam to exile—ends with an open door. Go up. Build. God is with you.

The Chronicler chose to end his book not with destruction but with restoration. Not with exile but with return. Not with judgment but with an invitation. The God who stirred the hearts of warriors to join David was now stirring the heart of a pagan emperor to release his people.

And notice who delivered the message of hope: not a prophet, not a priest, not a king from David's line, but a foreign emperor who didn't even worship Israel's God. Just as Hiram the Phoenician and the queen of Sheba had praised God at the height of Israel's glory, now Cyrus of Persia carried God's purposes at the moment of Israel's lowest point. God's plan had always been bigger than Israel, and even the rise and fall of empires couldn't stop it.

WHAT THIS MEANS FOR US

First, no one is beyond the reach of God's mercy. Manasseh committed every sin imaginable. He filled Jerusalem with blood and put idols in God's temple. And God forgave him because he humbled himself and prayed. If you think you've gone too far for God to reach you, Manasseh's story says otherwise. The door is open to anyone who comes with a humble heart.

Second, pride is the most dangerous sin because you can't see it in yourself. Uzziah was a great king. His success was real, his achievements were impressive, and his reign was long. But power made him think he was above the rules. Pride doesn't usually announce itself. It sneaks in after success and whispers that you don't need God the way you used to.

Third, God keeps working even when everything falls apart. The exile looked like the end. The temple was ashes.

The monarchy was over. But God stirred the heart of a Persian emperor, and the story continued. Whatever feels like the end in your life, God is not finished. He is always working, even through people and circumstances you'd never expect.

Fourth, the invitation is always open. The last words of Chronicles are an invitation: "Go up. God is with you." That's how the Chronicler chose to end his book. Not with a lecture. Not with a warning. With an open door and a blessing. No matter where you've been or what you've done, God's final word is never condemnation. It's an invitation to come home.

TALKING POINTS

1. **Uzziah's downfall came after years of success, when he "became powerful" and his "pride led to his downfall."** Why is success sometimes more spiritually dangerous than failure? How can you guard against pride when things are going well?

2. **The northern soldiers in Ahaz's time clothed, fed, and returned the captives they had taken from Judah—a story only found in Chronicles.** Why do you think the Chronicler included this? What does it teach about compassion toward enemies?

3. **Hezekiah prayed that God would pardon northerners who had come to the Passover without being ceremonially clean, and God healed them.** What does this tell you about the relationship between God's rules and God's grace? How do you hold both together?

4. **Manasseh was the worst king in Judah's history, yet when he humbled himself, God restored him. His son Amon committed the same sins but refused to humble him-**

self. What made the difference? Why is humility so central to God's response?

5. **The very last words of Chronicles are an invitation: "Any of his people among you may go up, and may the Lord their God be with them."** Why do you think the Chronicler chose to end his book this way? What does it tell you about what God wants his people to know above all else?

The story of Chronicles ends where it began: with God's faithfulness stretching across the centuries, from Adam to Abraham to David to exile and beyond. The temple was gone, but the promise wasn't. The throne was empty, but the King was coming. And the invitation that closed the book still echoes today: come home. God is with you.